LADY DIVERSITY POWER

WHY DIVERSITY IS THE NEW WAY TO DO BUSINESS

CURATED BY

Hazel Herrington and *Karen Mc Dermott*

NATIONAL LIBRARY OF AUSTRALIA   A catalogue record for this
work is available from the
National Library of Australia

National Library of Australia Catalogue-in-Publication data:

Lady Diversity Power/Hazel Herrington & Karen McDermott

ISBN:
978-0-6456278-2-4
(Paperback)

ISBN:
978-0-6456765-6-3
(Ebook)

Contents

Foreword

HE Laila Rahhal ELAFFANI

Dear readers,

The business world is changing. The days of the white, middle-aged man running the show are coming to an end. In their place, we're seeing a new kind of leader: one who understands and values diversity.

This is especially true in the world of work. Companies that want to thrive in the future must embrace diversity, both internally and externally. Why? Because a diverse workplace is a productive workplace.

Diversity isn't just about race or gender; it's about including different perspectives, backgrounds and ideas. When everyone in a company feels like they can be themselves, they're more likely to be creative and innovative. They're also more likely to be engaged and motivated, which leads to better performance overall.

So, what does the future of work look like? It looks like a world where diversity is celebrated and embraced. A world where people are encouraged to be their authentic selves. A world where all voices are heard.

We are living in a time of great change. Rapid advances in technology and globalisation are transforming the way we live and work. In this rapidly changing world, diversity is more important than ever.

Hazel Herrington and Karen McDermott have curated an excellent collection of essays that explore the importance of diversity in the workplace. This book is a valuable resource for anyone who wants to understand the future of work and diversity.

The essays in this book provide a wealth of information and insights about the importance of diversity. The contributors include leaders in business, government, academia and the non-profit sector. They share their experiences and offer their insights on how diversity can help businesses achieve success.

Why Diversity is the New Way of Doing Business

Hazel Herrington

Migrant women and African women frequently face unique challenges that are not often understood or appreciated in the business world. I wrote this book to help educate people about the importance of diversity in business, and to share my own story and experiences as a migrant woman and African woman in business.

I migrated to Australia from Africa over eight years ago and I have experienced firsthand the importance of diversity in business. When I first started my own business here in Australia, I was met with a lot of resistance from people who didn't understand or appreciate my culture or my background. Challenges that migrant businesswomen face include lack of access to capital, discrimination in the workplace and gender inequality. Additionally, I have lacked the necessary networks to help me grow my business. I have had to learn how to build these networks myself, which has been a difficult process. These challenges can be frustrating and discouraging, but I refused to give up and I worked hard to build my business into what it is today.

When I set out to write *Lady Diversity Power*, I did so for one primary reason: to help empower women entrepreneurs. It's no secret that women continue to face challenges when it comes to starting and running businesses. From accessing capital to being taken seriously in male-dominated industries, women have a lot working against them. But the good news is that things are changing.

Diversity is the New Way to do Business

As a migrant woman and African woman, I am passionate about promoting diversity in the workplace. Migrant women and African women bring a unique perspective to the table, and our voices need to be heard in the business world. We have a lot to offer, and we can contribute a great deal to the success of any organisation.

However, promoting diversity isn't always easy. There are many challenges that we face as migrant women and African women in business, but we can't let those challenges stop us from achieving our goals. We need to stand together and support one another, and we need to continue fighting for our rights in the workplace.

There is a growing movement of women who are determined to succeed, and they are finding ways to do so by leveraging the power of diversity. Diversity is not only good for business, it's essential for success. When businesses embrace diversity, they open themselves up to new ideas, perspectives and ways of thinking that can help them grow and thrive.

Despite the clear benefits, many businesses still struggle with inclusion and diversity issues. The reason for this is often because people find it difficult to talk about these topics. We all have our own biases and preconceived notions which makes it challenging to have open and honest conversations about diversity. But we need to have these conversations if we want to make progress.

So, what can be done to improve diversity in the workplace? Here are a few suggestions:

1. Educate yourself and your team about the benefits of diversity.

The benefits of diversity are vast and important. Diversity can improve problem-solving, creativity and communication. Additionally, diversity can lead to increased innovation and a better understanding of the customer base. Some examples of businesses that have benefitted from diversity initiatives are Google, PepsiCo and Marriott International.

Google is known for its innovative search engine algorithm and for being a global leader in technology. However, what many people don't know is that Google's success is due in part to its focus on diversity. In 2006, Google launched its 'Women in Engineering' program to increase the number of women in the company's engineering workforce. The program was a success, and over time Google has hired more women engineers, improved the working environment for them and increasing the number of women on the management team. As a result, Google has been able to create innovative products that appeal to a wide range of consumers.

In 2012, PepsiCo appointed Indra Nooyi as its CEO. Nooyi is Indian-American and had previously worked at PepsiCo for over twenty years. Under her leadership, PepsiCo made a number of changes to its business model including expanding its product portfolio to include healthier options and increasing its focus on marketing to multicultural audiences. As a result of these changes, PepsiCo has seen growth in both its revenue and profit margins.

Marriott has long been committed to hiring employees from diverse backgrounds and cultures. In fact, one-third of Marriott's employees are from minority groups. This commitment has paid off for them; the company's hotels have become known for their ethnic cuisine options and for their focus on customer service. Additionally, Marriott's diversity initiatives have helped the company to better understand its customer base and to create products that appeal to a wider range of people.

2. Be aware of your own biases and work to overcome them.

It is important to be aware of your own biases and work to overcome them. This includes acknowledging when you may have a personal stake in the matter at hand, or when you may have formed an opinion without all the facts. Oftentimes, we let our personal biases cloud our judgement and this can lead to inaccurate conclusions or decisions.

There are a number of ways to overcome personal biases. One approach is to seek out additional information and perspectives in order to get a more complete picture. Another option is to try to detach yourself emotionally from the issue at hand in order to make a more objective decision. Additionally, it can be helpful to reflect on your own beliefs and assumptions in order to identify any potential biases. Finally, it is important to be aware of the danger of groupthink which can lead individuals to conform to the consensus view, even if it is not accurate.

3. Foster a culture of inclusion in your workplace.

In order to foster a culture of inclusion in your workplace, you should first understand what it is. Inclusion is the active effort to welcome and include all individuals, regardless of their differences. This includes, but is not limited to, race, ethnicity, gender identity, sexual orientation, socioeconomic status, religion, age and abilities. Creating a culture of inclusion requires a commitment from all members of an organisation to embrace and respect everyone's differences.

There are many benefits to fostering a culture of inclusion in your workplace. First and foremost, it makes your workplace more diverse and inclusive which can lead to new perspectives and innovative ideas. A study by Deloitte found that companies with greater diversity outperform those without it. Additionally, a diverse and inclusive workplace is more likely to attract top talent. Employees want to work for organisations that celebrate diversity and support inclusion.

There are many ways you can foster a culture of inclusion in your workplace. The most important thing is to make sure everyone in the organisation is onboard with the idea and committed to creating a welcoming environment for all. You can start by setting clear expectations for behaviour and creating policies that support diversity and inclusion. You can also provide training for all employees. This will help them understand what it means and how they can contribute to creating a more inclusive environment. Finally, be sure to celebrate diversity and inclusion in everything you do. Make sure everyone feels welcome and appreciated for their contributions.

4. Promote diversity and inclusion initiatives from the top down.

Top-down diversity and inclusion initiatives create a company culture that values and respects all individuals. This type of culture is inclusive and employees feel safe to be themselves and share their unique perspectives. A study by the Society for

Human Resource Management found that nearly nine in ten organisations have diversity and inclusion initiatives, and that these programs improve employee engagement, creativity and productivity.

Some examples of top-down diversity and inclusion initiatives include executive training on unconscious bias, sponsorship and mentorship programs for under-represented groups and employee resource groups. By implementing these types of programs, organisations can send a clear message that they value a diverse and inclusive workplace.

5. Encourage employees to speak up about any issues they encounter related to diversity and inclusion.

Employees who feel comfortable speaking up about issues they encounter related to diversity and inclusion can create an environment where those issues can be addressed head-on. This can improve the workplace for everyone involved.

According to a study by the Society for Human Resource Management, 'diversity and inclusion are critical to organisational success.' The study found that, 'companies with a more diverse workforce perform better financially and are better equipped to meet the needs of a changing customer base.'

There are many examples of organisations that have succeeded because of their commitment to diversity and inclusion. Inclusion improves an organisation's ability to innovate and come up with new ideas, which is essential in today's economy.

Women Entrepreneurs are Powerful

When we invited other women from diverse backgrounds and cultures to co-author this book, we did so with the power of networking and collaboration amongst women in mind. I believe that when we come together, we can create powerful change.

Women entrepreneurs are powerful. They are powerful because they have the ability to create change. They have the ability to create change in their own lives, in the lives of their families and in the lives of their communities. Women entrepreneurs come from diverse backgrounds and cultures, and they use their power to make a difference.

For example, consider the story of Karen Finney. Karen is the co-founder of digitalundivided, a social enterprise that is dedicated to increasing the number of women of colour in technology entrepreneurship. As a woman entrepreneur, Karen has used her power to create change. She has created a space for other women of colour to pursue their dreams in technology and she has shown them that they can achieve anything they set their minds to.

Or consider the story of Uma Valeti. Uma is the co-founder and CEO of Memphis Meats, a company that is working to create meat from stem cells. As a woman entrepreneur, Uma has used her power to create change. She has shown the world that it is possible to create meat without harming any animals and she has demonstrated that it is possible to create sustainable food products that are good for both people and the planet.

Women have a unique power to connect with each other and to share our stories. We can use our stories to build empathy, understanding and connection. We can also use them to inspire others to take action. This book will have a powerful impact on society because it has women co-authoring from various races. Our voices will be amplified and heard by many. Our stories will help to break down barriers and unite us all in the pursuit of equality and justice.

When it comes to the world of business, diversity is the new way to do things. You can't succeed in today's marketplace without being diverse and inclusive in your thinking. This book explores how businesses can become more diverse and inclusive and offers real-world examples of how to make this happen.

If you're looking to stay ahead of the competition, then you need to read this book. It will show you how to embrace diversity and inclusion in your business and help you stay ahead of the curve. Not only will this make your business more successful, but it will also make it a more welcoming place for everyone. So, what are you waiting for?

Hazel Herrington

Hazel is a multiple-award-winning entrepreneur who has spent a decade empowering women and youth to become economically independent and wholly sufficient worldwide. She has recently been crowned the Top 100 most successful women in the world and won the 2022 Entrepreneurship Award at the National Migrant Achiever awards in Australia. She was also honoured with the World Greatness Award by Greatness University in the United Kingdom and nominated for the Australia Top 100 Women of Influence Award.

Hazel is also a successful board advisor, author and entrepreneur, having founded and led several businesses to success. She is the founder and CEO of Herrington Publications Worldwide, a publishing and marketing company that produces the popular inspiring magazines *I Am Woman Global, Lady Global Power* and *Lady Politico Power* which are distributed in over 130 countries to over 25 million viewers on pressreader.com

Hazel has been an invaluable resource to women all over the world, providing them with the tools and resources they need to achieve their dreams. Her expertise is in the areas of business and leadership development, women's empowerment, marketing and entrepreneurship.

Hazel is a powerful international speaker, sharing her story of overcoming adversity to inspire others to reach their full potential. She has spoken at numerous conferences and events around the world which include the following:

- Forbes School of Business & Technology, International Women's Day with the former President of Mauritius HE Madame President Dr Ameenah Gurib-Fakim.
- The Pearls of Africa Women Leadership Conference held by Berkeley Middle East Holdings and hosted by the Royal Family Investment Advisor Musa Shaik.
- 'Achieving SDGs through entrepreneurship and innovation' Women Entrepreneurship Congress 2020 held by Female Innovators Hub with the former President of Mauritius HE Madame President Dr Ameenah Gurib-Fakim.
- NAC 2018 Australia with Tony Robbins.
- B Squared 2017 Australia with Gary Vee.

It Starts With a 'Why'

Annie Gibbins

I was recently asked why I chose to create Women's Biz Tribe and to become a global women's empowerment coach. As I searched for my reply, I activated one of my key drivers.

It was at that moment the answer became glaringly obvious to me. At the very core of my 'why' is that I choose to remain uncomfortable about gender inequality, and I am committed to being a part of the long-term solution.

Gender inequality is not acceptable, it never has been. In fact, it serves no value at all. Behind every decision I make, I ask myself, *Is this helping or hindering my 'why' – my purpose?* Fundamentally, I believe that 50% of the population should have 50% of the available opportunities, and more importantly, 100% of the rights and entitlements they deserve.

Women across the world deserve safety, security, health, wealth, education and freedom. But deserving and receiving are not simple to achieve. The world has undergone scrutiny at the hands of a pandemic, a war and an economic backlash. The current issues plaguing the world are a tragedy and should not be normalised. My greatest fear is that we stop advocating for a gender equal world, whilst attending to one tragedy after the next.

It begs the question, how would the devastating war and conflict between Russia and Ukraine play out if more women were behind the scenes at senior levels?

I am willing to bet a great deal better.

It is when we accept the unacceptable that we reduce our capacity to build the fabric of society we require.

As both my grandmothers used to say, 'You reap what you sow,' and we need to sow with our future generations, with a soul purpose that drives humanity to lift its game.

We continue to identify the issues of gender equality, set government agendas and rally with society for a better world, but the gender tragedies continue. We continue to see the horrific aftermaths of war, sex trafficking, unwanted teenage pregnancy, poverty, genital mutilation, violence and the forever lingering gender pay gap disparity.

Currently in Australia, the national gender pay gap is 13.8%. This percentage needs to shift north. As a C-suite leader, podcast host and number-one bestselling author, I am passionate about how to debunk myths and educate women on how to transform their professional career with a seven-figure mindset. As an influencer and entrepreneur, I know it's all about *what* you know, *who* you know and *how* you overcome challenges.

Triumph becomes possible when you focus on creating synergic opportunities that build their own momentum and make the painful aspects of your business more pleasurable. In my experience, I have demonstrated that a growth mindset and love for innovation, automation and collaboration are essential ingredients to enhance the results of tried and tested formulas.

But my success didn't get handed to me on a plate. I worked hard for every accolade, pay packet and job title I received, because I am a self-confessed go-getter, who can function with just six hours of sleep a night. This pace isn't for everyone. In fact, I recommend taking as much downtime as your health and lifestyle requires. What I do know is that playing it safe doesn't launch you to the stars.

With three university degrees under my belt, I am now a go-to inspirational speaker globally for women leaders in business. As founder of The Women's Business Incubator and The Women's Business Tribe, I am a digital powerhouse helping to push the limits of what is truly possible.

Starting my career as a registered nurse, I went on to become a health educationist, change management CEO and entrepreneur whilst raising my family of five including two sets of twins born twenty-six months apart. After graduating with a Diploma of Health Science and working as a registered nurse, my thirst for professional development continued, leading me to complete a Master of Education, business and management qualifications.

Proudly positioned as one of Australia's leading voices for women in business, I am an advocate for female leadership in business. As recognised in the 'Top Women's Change Maker 2021', my passion for gender equality is unwavering when it comes to excelling the potential of the female workforce.

So, it goes without saying, what are our next steps in achieving this?

We Need to Get Uncomfortable with the Facts

According to the [1]'High Journal Publication', 25 million people across the globe are denied their fundamental right to freedom.

---

1 thehighcourt.co/human-trafficking-statistics

The alarming and depressing statistic shows that 30% of the global human trafficking victims are children. Out of the reported victims, 1,290 were female, 149 were male and ten were gender minorities. These startling statistics lean heavily on the gender imbalance and the fact that trafficked victims are predominantly female. In 2019, 62% of victims in the US were identified as sex trafficking victims.

The key issues affecting women have been a constant issue throughout history. This status quo has been seen as, if not acceptable, then sadly realistic, and even dare I say, inevitable.

These things are not inevitable.

They are not acceptable.

They should never have *become* acceptable.

So, we need to remain uncomfortable until we no longer need to speak about gender inequality. We need to champion equal representation in all key areas of influence around the world.

As poetic as hope is, hope is not enough. Hope does not shift perspectives at the rate hope needs to. Hope does not encourage a woman, downtrodden by abuse and neglect. Hope is love, and hope is a dream we should all cling to, but hope won't get to the change-makers that matter. We need actionable and tangible solutions.

We need to be unapologetic about using our voices to demand a higher standard. We need to provide solutions that work for the betterment of society. We need to unite with a narrative that inspires, empowers and equips.

We can do better, each and every one of us.

So how do we, as business leaders, break through the barriers that are currently designed to inhibit us from achieving equal success?

We must clearly articulate the issues that are compounding

the progress to change: cost, impact and disparity.

You see, when you clearly identify and accept a problem, you can then take intentional steps to collectively solve it. It's integral that we create a strategy that is purpose driven. Be strategic and purpose driven. I reiterate, we need to get uncomfortable first, to desire enough discomfort to drive mindset shifts that have been formed, validated and even championed for over hundreds of years.

When we have arrived at a not-so-comfy reality, we need to measure our success and that needs data.

Recently, the [2]Workplace Gender Equality Agency produced a scorecard representing 4 million Australian employees, or 40% of the workforce. The data painted a picture of the current reality, and it challenged me to stay uncomfortable. Despite women being more highly educated and comprising 47.4% of all employed persons, women are just not making the cut.

The report findings were undisputable and terrifying.

Men are twice as likely as women to be in the top earnings quartile, earning $120,000 and above, while women are 50% more likely than men to be in the bottom quartile, earning $60,000 and less. The data reports that women earn 14.2% less than men for comparable jobs. That's $25,800 less in the bank, resulting in 23.4% less superannuation at retirement.

The gender gap is very real and very unacceptable.

When 47.4% of the workforce constitutes 67.6% of all part-time employees and the lion's share of casual positions, there will be significant consequences when a global pandemic hits – and it did.

My Theory About Juggling Babies,

2 wgea.gov.au/sites/default/files/documents/2020-21_WGEA_SCORECARD.pdf

Boardrooms and Billion-Dollar Budgets

We need women in leadership positions so their voices can be heard and their value recognised. Yes, we want to be equally represented in the boardrooms that matter, but more than that we want to be equally represented in chair and executive positions. Targeted positions of power and influence.

Only eighteen women are among the CEOs of Australia's largest three hundred companies, or 6.2%, according to the [3]2021 Chief Executive Women Senior Executive Census.

Australia's leading publication, [4]*The Sydney Morning Herald,* reported only one woman was promoted to the role of chief executive out of twenty-five appointments at Australia's largest companies over the past year, a sign gender equality in the professional world is going backwards.

So now you can see why I was driven and determined to create The Women's Business Incubator, which helps women to startup, scaleup and dominate in business. To ensure they will be well equipped to be placed in positions of power and influence in all levels of decision-making globally.

I choose to let my wounds become my superpowers. I choose to always herald my family in every keynote speech. I am unafraid to be a woman in a budget meeting, and have no problem wearing multiple hats, because essentially, it's one big, phenomenal hat. And we can all wear them if we choose.

I want to empower women to value their worth, and this can be achieved. We do this by speaking out, providing workable solutions, supporting each other to ensure our foundations are strong and our voice unified.

---

3 cew.org.au/topics/cew-senior-executive-census
4 smh.com.au/business/companies/absolutely-no-progress-number-of-female-ceos-in-australia-is-declining-20200916-p55w5m.html

A research study from the [5]University of Chicago reported two major reasons for women's under-representation. Firstly, the 'election aversion', or women just not wanting to run for a seat in parliament. Do we really question why this is the case? The second reason for governmental under-representation by women, is voter bias against female candidates, which, they believe, still exists.

I think we can all safely agree that it does.

And I can tell you it is so much more than that!

Data captured by [6]UN Women suggests, at the current rate, gender equality in the highest positions of power will not be reached for another 130 years.

Currently, just thirteen countries have a woman head of government. As a gender diverse advocate, I am currently working to unite and empower individuals and organisations who are working to achieve United Nation's sustainable development goal number five: gender equality and inclusion.

We must be bold, brave and practice what we preach!

If we continue our struggle to employ and inspire women to seek education, to explore professional expansion and remove the gender defaults when faced with a crisis, our political leaders will not be representative of those they serve.

The Comeback of the COVID-19 Lost Leaders

Just when the conversation was heating up about gender equality and the disproportionate pay gap between male and female co-workers, the global pandemic reversed the efforts of progress for women in the workplace.

In years to come, psychologists, researchers, economic masterminds and educators will study those who lived through

5 harris.uchicago.edu/news-events/news/beating-bias-why-women-make-better-candidates-and-members-congress
6 unwomen.org/en/what-we-do/leadership-and-political-participation/facts-and-figures

COVID-19. They will hold our governments and economists under scrutiny and study the societal response to the virus that shut down the world overnight. The coronavirus outbreak has dismantled health, economy and social norms in a blink of an eye.

When the pandemic triggered a global economic fallout, COVID-19 showed us that women were the first to lose their jobs. Millions of women downed tools to self-sacrifice their success, to homeschool children alone. Sadly, we saw the devastating rise of domestic violence, which spiked four times greater versus five years ago.

We need to remain very uncomfortable about this.

When your income, opportunities and spirit have been impacted so significantly, it makes it extremely unlikely that you will be mentally and physically positioned to influence positive change. The infamous [7]Maslow's Hierarchy of Needs taught us that you cannot operate at the optimal capacity when your core needs are threatened. Newsflash, they are being threatened.

So, while we need to celebrate the progress we have made to reduce the barriers and bias that have negatively impacted women's rights, the world continues to be deprived when 50% of the population are not represented when decisions are being made.

For many women, the coronavirus pandemic has forced them back into traditional gender roles. As COVID-19 continues to infiltrate the world's economy, women are facing little choice when it comes to prioritising domestic security over success. Despite the world opening again, the international fallout for women in business is at serious threat. Are we looking at gender regression versus the efforts of gender recognition?

According to McKinsey and Company, women's jobs are [8]1.8

7 simplypsychology.org/maslow.html
8 mckinsey.com/featured-insights/future-of-work/covid-19-and-gender-equality-countering-the-re-gressive-effects

times more vulnerable to this crisis than men's jobs. Women make up 39% of global employment but account for 54% of overall job losses. Despite the women and men diluting employment across multiple sectors, women's unemployment is dropping rapidly.

The reason behind this significant decline during the pandemic is the overwhelming burden for women to bear the brunt of unpaid child care. As child care centres and schools battened down the hatches in the height of the pandemic, the roles within the household sadly defaulted back to a scenario unfavoured for women earning their bread.

As a result of COVID-19, typically mothers are spending an extra hour each day on unpaid housework and four extra hours on child care. It has been noted that fathers are expending about half of that effort, putting in only an extra thirty minutes on housework and two additional hours on child care during the crisis. Essentially, women at work are picking up the slack despite the professional demands being no different.

Likewise, women are clearly upping the ante when it comes to unpaid work at home. Preliminary survey results by Dr Brendan Churchill and colleagues at [9]The University of Melbourne suggests the gender gap is widening.

Parents have faced their most difficult choices yet. Often, the burden falls on the mother. For those sitting in the precarious position of 'how can I have it all?', women are submitting their resignations faster than men. Not only does the economy suffer, but any advancements made for women to excel in leadership roles massively dips. A study conducted in the UK suggests that [10]46% of mothers that have been made redundant during the pandemic cite lack of adequate child care as the cause.

9 onlinelibrary.wiley.com/doi/full/10.1111/gwao.12484
10 lordslibrary.parliament.uk/covid-19-empowering-women-in-the-recovery-from-the-impact-of-the-pandemic

It was noted that 70% of women with caring responsibilities who requested furlough following school closures in 2021 had their request denied. This has led to almost half of working mothers (48%) being worried about negative treatment from an employer because of child care responsibilities. Whilst the virus was unpredicted, our professionals' infrastructures have been grossly underprepared to protect those facing demotions, unfair dismissals and inevitable job losses.

With no action taken to address the effects of unemployment for women, it is estimated that global value added to the economy growth could be $1 trillion lower in 2030 than it would be if women's unemployment simply tracked that of men in each sector.

Women account for the hardest hit in specific sectors, with some of the highest COVID-19 job losses, such as retail, accommodation, food and customer services. The skewed irony when it comes to employment demands during a pandemic are the heroes on our frontlines.

Nurses, doctors, health care workers and paramedics have undoubtedly risen to the challenge in employment adversity. Many other frontline workers, including teachers, early childhood educators and aged care professionals have taken care of our young and supported our elderly. For every positive COVID-19 result, a child is at risk, a classroom is closed and school gates chained. Predominantly these occupations employ women, so with communities in lockdown means less women in the workplace.

Women in business across the economic footprint of diversity suggests the road to recognition and recovery is going to be long. We know that the global pandemic has clearly taken its toll on all of us. We are facing and will continue to observe the aftermath of what has been an unprecedented time. The mental exhaustion for those attempting to do it all is more prevalent than ever.

A report released by [11]McKinsey and Company, titled *Women in the Workplace 2021*, recognised that during a year and a half into the COVID-19 pandemic, mothers and women in senior positions have felt more pressure, exhaustion and burnout in the workplace than men. They are also more likely to have their judgement questioned, be mistaken for someone more junior and be the victim of demeaning remarks. With only 8% of women accounting for C-suite roles, women leaders need to strategise their comeback more than ever.

Change Starts with Us

Instead of having a front row seat to change, we must change the narrative among all of us.

It's simple but true: mindset matters. Did you know, the human brain processes approximately 90,000 thoughts per day? How we direct our attitude will be cemented by each of those thoughts. If your tank is running on red, or your belief system is 'my life is a glass half empty', then you are cementing failure after failure.

As an advocate and leader, I see failures as wins. Without them, we don't learn and reconstruct ways to do a better job next time. To be leaders, we need to innovate, and we all know any invented prototype rarely works on the first go. So, get ready to become more tenacious as seeing a failure and believing we are failures are juxtaposed perspectives.

As an advocate for education, I encourage my children, teams and clients to keep learning. Never close a book or turn off a podcast if information is still being absorbed. But education is only part of the jigsaw puzzle, as our mindset and limiting beliefs are constantly at play in the background. We need to continually work on exploring our unconscious mind as often we aren't even aware that we are betting for a bad day.

---

11 mckinsey.com/featured-insights/diversity-and-inclusion/women-in-the-workplace

To succeed in business, here are some key tips and tricks that helped me along the way:

Seek out positive influences: Intentionally seeking out positive influences or people in your life is paramount to creating a kickass mindset. When you start interacting in an environment that inspires, equips and empowers you to rise, you will achieve what you thought was previously impossible. They will teach you how to dream big and act bigger.

Swim with the tide: Many of us at times feel like we are swimming against the tide which is exhausting and takes effort that is better spent elsewhere. To go with the flow, you need to find workable solutions instead of resisting change. It can feel scary and make you feel uncomfortable, however, when you push through and learn to ride a new wave, you may find situations that have been designed perfectly for you to learn, grow and triumph.

Strive to be positive: Positive people bring joy, happiness and uplifting energy, plus they are fun to be around, and what's not to love about that? While it's not realistic to be positive all the time, it is possible most of the time. It is how we respond to situations that matters, and you can do this with a positive attitude while feeling the depth of your emotions and remaining wise and responsive to risk.

When you start looking closely, there are positives to find in almost every situation, even the challenging ones. Once you shift your mindset towards 'how can I help?' or 'what can I do?', you will become more motivated to lean into your true potential.

Don't forget you are dealing with humans: Our emotional intelligence is not emotional, and we need it more than ever. Modern business requires us to connect with people in a personal way as we are measured by how we respond to their specific needs. As leaders, we need to inspire and not just venture onto a one-woman journey to the bank. Whilst the bottom line is everything, humanness is needed more than ever. So, as you juggle, create, sell and manage, try to engage a leadership style that embraces collective thought, engagement and ownership.

Together we achieve more.

How to Keep Kicking on When Life Itself Has Kicked You

Like most people, I have a pet hate of the word 'busy'. So often when I ask someone 'how was your day?' and 'how is business?', they respond with the same two words, 'I'm busy'. Not that I want to teach anyone to suck eggs, but being busy is not a state of mind, but a very commonly used verb. For so long we have believed that a quarterly burnout is a sign of success.

That if we work twelve-hour days, somehow, we 'have it all'. This can be a dangerous mindset for any leader. When we apply more systematic processes, and not the qualities we once deemed were key, then we have a better chance of balance (and who doesn't want more balance in their lives?).

Raising a family of five, climbing the corporate ladder and launching my own business came with its fair share of chaos. As a self-confessed adrenaline junkie with a thirst for success, I know that knockbacks are part of the course for women striving for reward and recognition. As a mother, woman and female leader, I deem it my responsibility to carve out a better future around gender diversity.

Gender equality is not shifting, despite it making the headlines for decades. The foundation for an equal, perceptively challenged sustainable world is tipping the scales of gender mindsets. Despite the progress of gender recognition, many challenges remain, and the largest is if women and girls are safe in our current world.

To be a global women's empowerment coach, I want to empower future generations of women to campaign for their own change. Women are continually being challenged, not because it exudes a strength, because it's a test to see if they can. Data and statistics have proven that one in five women and girls between the ages of fifteen and forty-nine report experiencing physical or sexual violence by an intimate partner within a twelve-month period.

These figures are cascading in a world already in turmoil and it's our job, as women on the frontline in economic growth, to ensure that no-one, kicked down or otherwise, is left behind.

Charity and Activism – How to Build a Purpose From Scratch

As the former CEO of Glaucoma Australia, an organisation dedicated to providing sight-saving education, support and advocacy to people with glaucoma, I am no stranger on how to maximise impact on a shoestring. I personally secured the Governor-General of Australia as patron and then rockstars Kirk Pengilly (INXS) and David Koch (*Sunrise* TV show host) as ambassadors. I know how to manage teams of experts to provide 20,000+ patients education via an innovative patient support journey I personally designed.

Coming from a background in health and education, I am passionate about providing interventions that promote wellness. While not every charity has the initial finance to make a tangible impact, when you combine purpose and passion with strong business principles, a magic formula starts to activate. Once you know how to effectively 'share the good news', you will find yourself attracting other prospects like bees to honey.

Currently, I hold advisory roles on several boards, and my expertise to raise funds at national and international levels has enabled so many causes to do what they do best: advocate. Many of my clients come to me with a big idea.

They are successful businesswomen at senior executive levels, but they want to do more. Some have been touched personally by a trauma, whilst others simply have a desire to give back. The reason advocacy and activism exist is because they have discovered their 'why'.

Identifying your 'why' is key. In the world of advocacy, building from the ground up will establish your purpose. This could, in fact, apply to any ambition. But when we are in the thick of a business brainstorm, we don't always see the ideas that are often staring us in the face. Inspired by working with women ranging from startup devotees to CEOs on a seven-figure salary, I am an objective cheerleader with a front row seat, taking a concept into a go-live brand.

Like anything, when you are creating a purpose – be it a relationship, a family or business – going back to basics is everything. I urge all women who read this to identify your purpose with conviction, evaluate its sustainability, create uplifting content, pitch your plan and connect with a powerhouse network who will never leave your side.

Myth-Debunking — What People Don't Realise

Like fear, myths about business have a nasty way of working themselves into a 'success building bootcamp'. Much like the unhelpful download of fake news, there are many myths that catapult an idea into the too-hard basket. Before we know it, we have parked our plans for growth and find ourselves back on the slow train we have been riding for years.

Glossy magazines will always, and should, showcase the success stories that sell. But being an entrepreneur and woman in business can also be a calamity of errors. In my thirty years of business while juggling five children, home and after-school activity clubs, I navigated the slips, trips and overwhelm that goes with giving entrepreneurship a red-hot go.

As one of Australia's leading business influencers, I am here to tell you the myths that need debunking and how to keep them exactly where they belong, in your desktop recycle bin.

I'm not an expert: As I always say, you are the expert of your experiences. If you are ready to take the next step in building your success, trust that you have the skills and services needed at hand.

No-one is going to be more passionate about your brand than you. And what you don't know, you will learn ... and fast. Every CEO, senior leader and global ambassador has learnt on the job and been one foot in front of their audience. But their biggest attribute is their instinct. Tap into that and you will be your own expert in no time.

People won't buy from me when they have Google: We are a generation that needs 'instant everything'. We want a movie, we go to Netflix. We want a meal, we head to Uber Eats. We want love, we swipe on Tinder. Many have no patience or capacity to find the answers if it will take longer than five minutes. The compelling part of your brand is that you are delivering what Google cannot: hearty experience.

Universities do not focus on the curriculum like they did, because any information found in a PowerPoint can now be found on the internet. Education institutions are now looking for something that cannot be found via SEO rankings – experience from the industry leaders and the networks. Don't compete with the internet but collaborate with your resources.

There are brands out there like mine: This is a good thing! This means that you are on track. Now, the task is discovering your uniqueness, your brand story and how you are going to tell it with originality and difference. The truth is, almost every single problem worth solving has already been tackled. Blogs, books and online courses exist, but there is only one of you. What makes you and your brand a stand-out?

Entrepreneurs can predict the future: This is somewhat true, but this statement is more about confidence in a vision than an entrepreneur's ability to time travel. Entrepreneurs, startups and powerhouse business moguls have an innate ability to see a gap in the untapped market. They identify an investment, product or service unlike any other, but their manifestation can often be mistaken for prediction.

Going it solo is your only option: Wrong. Whilst entrepreneurs are the visionary and solo flyer, they often rely on a suite of skills in the boardroom. As a coach, I mentor and champion my clients to believe in their wildest dreams. I am a devoted leader of businesses, where knowing the skills of her employees ensures that I can do my job better, and in turn, the company will excel.

Ego and entrepreneurship in healthy doses work but having an idea without a partner means accountability and prosperity can fall by the wayside.

Business success is the only success: Success is defined by a set of values and standards only you can access. For some, success is a seven-figure salary, for others, becoming a CEO after twenty years as a 2IC, and for others it's to get back into the workforce after a ten-year gap whilst raising the family.

As an advocate for gender equality, I am committed to ensuring all women and girls are included in any goal they set their sights on. It's our job as leaders to ensure diversity and success is defined by the woman that makes it, and it's accessible to all.

Lastly, I will leave you with this. To be in a position of power is a privilege.

And with privilege comes great responsibility to raise the bar on what is truly possible and necessary for all humanity.

Annie Gibbins

Starting her career as a registered nurse, Annie went on to become a health educationist, change management CEO and entrepreneur whilst raising her family of five, including two sets of twins born twenty-six months apart.

Annie Gibbins is a passionate and purpose-driven 'fempreneur', global women's empowerment coach, CEO, podcast host, speaker and number-one bestselling author.

Positioned as one of Australia's leading voices for women in leadership and founder of The Women's Business Incubator and The Women's Business Tribe, Annie is a digital powerhouse helping women push the limits of what is truly possible.

As G100 Australia Country Chair – Equity & Equality, her passion for gender equality is unwavering when it comes to excelling the potential of the female workforce. Annie is driven by demolishing the glass ceiling and removing the invisible barriers to success that many women come up against in their business and life journey.

As the host of *Memoirs of Successful Woman*, Annie has interviewed hundreds of inspirational women worldwide. Her continuous portfolio of high-calibre podcast guests range from business leaders, entrepreneurs, humanitarians, athletes and the creators of startups on a mission.

With three university degrees under her belt and twenty years of executive change management experience, Annie is now a go-to inspirational global speaker. In 2020, she earned the distinguished 'Unsung Business Hero' title in recognition of her formidable courage, compassion, perseverance, conviction and selflessness when coaching women to thrive. Speaking at the World Economic Forum, Annie shared the importance of engagement with political, business and cultural leaders to shape global, regional and industry agendas.

As a keynote speaker at the 'Lady America Power: Barriers and Bias, The Status of Women in Leadership' in 2021, Annie shared the power behind unlocking the visibility of female entrepreneurs around the globe. This prestigious event celebrated women internationally, heralding the importance of women in leadership.

Global brand, Hoinser Group, dedicated to promoting outstanding individuals in business throughout Europe, Africa, Asia, UAE and USA, invited Annie to their collective as an honourable member, elevating her influence tenfold.

Annie has graced covers and written articles for books and magazines including *1 Habit Leadership, I am Woman Global, Lady Speaker Power, Success, Hoinser, W, CIO Times,* and *MO2VATE Magazine.* She was named Top Women's Change Maker and Global Goodwill Ambassador in 2021.

Global Business Advisor
Cathy Dimarchos

Business is about impact and how you leave people after they have met you!

Knowing Where to Start

Knowing where to start is often the one thing that holds many women back. As a global business advisor, I have seen and heard it all, from brilliant minds to those who dare to dream. I share this because I want you know that you are not alone in the journey of doubt, lack of clarity and perhaps even self-sabotage; it is all possible and no challenge or obstacle will stand in your way when you have one key driver become crystal clear, and that is knowing the impact you want to make in the world.

I have very likely walked your path at some stage in my career, but as I write this chapter, I want you to know that you will have someone in your corner, someone shouting out your name in a room of opportunities and someone who believes in you even when you have moments of doubt, so give yourself permission to think big and reach for it because it is yours for the taking.

I have walked the path of entrepreneurship many times and scaled businesses, and have taken others with me each time. So have the courage to start your journey and then to ask for help when you feel you want to learn more, because you don't need to do it alone – it does not make you 'less than' by asking for help, in fact, if you allow others to rise alongside you, they get to share in the glory of being part of something bigger.

As a female, a mum, a daughter and a wife, I have had many thoughts in my life, yes including doubt, but not knowing where to start has seldom held me back. If I were to be honest, that is one thing that I know I can break down and make clear so that everyone involved knows how they can contribute. This is what I call part of my place of genius; I can create the starting point by knowing the end point. You see, I don't complicate things.

When we over complicate things, that is often the beginning of the internal dialogue that places us in the centre of a vortex that tends to hold us back. The 'how' is not always visible at the onset and this is why we diversify; collaborations are vital in life and in business.

Looking Back to Step Forward

As a young girl, I kept busy, I played lots of sport, I changed what I did with the seasons, I mixed across friendship groups, and it was all about following a passion and creating the space to fit it all in. So, when I look back, I realise this is in many ways why diversity and collaboration come so naturally to me. I was very competitive, but it did not mean that I kept things to myself, it was always about sharing tricks, tips and taking others on the journey with me.

I learnt from an early age that if I wanted to mix things up and do it all, it was possible, I just needed to be structured and most importantly I needed to know what I wanted to do just as much as what I didn't want to do. There was so much more joy when others were on the journey with me.

Diversity was about what I chose to include, not what others told me I should or could. In fact, if I recall correctly, it was seldom what others shared as 'this is how it's always been done'. I was raised to have courage and determination. It was not about what others were doing, but what I saw would either serve me or give me joy and what would help me to take others on the journey with me. Sure, I made mistakes, but they became the line in the sand that showed me what I could do differently the next time. It was the lessons that I took with me not the emotion of failing. There was always a solution or an alternative option and it was up to me to find out what that was. Business is no different. If you truly know the impact that you want to make in the world, you can create an environment that enables you to deliver the outcomes that you are seeking to make. I have been told many a time in my career that I could not do something or that others wouldn't see the value in what I did. It was often suggested that I do things 'their way', but in those moments, I saw and heard the opportunities that existed as I paused and listened for what was not said – which in many occasions was drowned in fear, theirs not mine – in doing something different.

Diversity exists around us, and in part we can create it, so being conscious and aware of how we might contribute enables us to bring about change – we don't need to wait for someone else to give us permission. We can step forward and despite the outcome, keep stepping forward to show others how they too can be part of the change. Dwelling on what others have said or done will not create the path we are seeking. In fact, if we do so, we continue to fuel their existence as we perpetuate from stepping into our own lane and doing things our way.

Being Prepared to Ask for Help Increases Diversity

I have been blessed with trust as people seek me out after they have been referred to me for counsel in their business. This takes courage, to share something that you have created and built. Knowing that there is something more that is needed by someone other than yourself, can create the same deep passion and desire to achieve success for someone else but this comes back to values and alignment, and when we begin to show trust, we begin to earn it too.

Trust is the centre of any relationship, be it personal or in business, and when we are prepared to give it, we are then creating the space for it to be earned, lived and shown.

This process of trust opens the doors and opportunities for diversity, and as strange as this may seem, it is often in sharing differences where we begin to create barriers. We have systems within systems, and whilst there are systems that may prevent equality, diversity, and acceptance, we too have in some ways contributed to these.

So often we seek out people like ourselves to guide and support us, and this is a pattern that we seldom recognise, but this creates exclusion – no matter who you are. We do it because it makes us feel safe and because it is familiar to us. These patterns keep us in our comfort zone, but also prevent us from being diverse. It also prevents us from growth because we will seldom be challenged in these situations. *Take a moment to reflect upon this.* Do you choose to seek out help from someone you think will challenge you – someone that will stretch you? Or do you ask for feedback from someone you feel safe with and deep down you know you feel comfortable to share with? It is fine if you choose the safe path, we have all done this and it is the reason why I share this familiar pattern, so you begin to ask how you contribute to diversity.

We all need differences to grow, but first we must begin to recognise our own patterns and beliefs and make a choice in how we want to contribute. Recognising this about ourselves is the beginning of growth and is beginning to break the systems that we have control of.

Creating impact, celebrating differences and breaking through ceilings is about doing what others have not yet done, and this means you are encouraged and excited to look outside your circle. This means that you are prepared to seek input and feedback from someone you would normally think was different and that will challenge you.

Interesting – maybe even controversial? But here it is; being prepared to do things differently to what you know and what you have always done in life and in business allows you also to include diversity. It is through differences that we create diversity so let's begin our journey in business by creating a space to think outside the box.

Identity begins with you knowing who you are and who you choose to be. If you choose to be inclusive, you begin the cycle with asking, 'What else?'

Taking the First Step

This can be very simple. Know what you don't want just as much as what you do want. Set clear boundaries that allow you to centre your business on values. When these are in alignment, you are accepting yourself for the person that is prepared to make the impact you are setting out to achieve. This takes you to a higher vibration and reverberates a ripple effect outward that then bounces back with universal feedback.

Whilst my business is about helping others succeed and in creating a sustainable and scalable business, it is all based on values, boundaries, alignment and potential in people with the intention of paying things forward. In everything I do, it is about supporting our future generation, with a focus on developing countries so that as a collective our future leaders begin to shape a better tomorrow.

The programs that I have developed under our Raise the Base-line Programs are aimed at showing children various 'leadership' qualities, tips and tools starting at the age of twelve through to young aspiring entrepreneurs so that they can begin their journey in life from a higher place than where they began. These programs are about reducing poverty, elevating humanity and providing education and knowledge so that they can contribute to their future and the planet we live in.

If you are a woman who wants to be an entrepreneur, or is already in business, you have the power to create your own inclusive and diverse path.

Knowing the impact you want to make with what you do is the key. There is no need to follow a story that someone has created for you as your story and the road you want to take will be the journey that will break through barriers and enable you to surge forward despite challenges and obstacles. This courage enables you to look beyond hurdles, but most importantly it allows you to find solutions when things become difficult.

It is this process that I work with when I help clients whose values align with mine and who know that they want more from life and more for humanity. Creating a road map and providing tangible tools and skills that are suitable for each person, each team and each business is critical to the success and sustainability of a business, and this is why I do what I do.

I don't work with cookie-cutter processes or models, and I choose my clients with as much care as they choose me. For me, it is important in every process to initially pause and better understand the person or the business so that we may ensure that our values are aligned, and once these are shared, it would be a privilege to share knowledge that may challenge them and elevate them so that they begin to see and trust in the impact that can be made. We begin your story with the lens that comes from you. This process begins with foundations that enable you to build, scale and then make sound decisions with you holding the power. At the core remains your values and the acceptance of inclusion of differences so that we may continue to be part of the change.

The Power of Holistic Knowledge

Knowledge brings power, challenges bring growth and differences bring inclusion, and when we begin with all of these in mind, we build from solid foundations to ensure that what we say and what we do align.

We all start with our skills and passion followed quickly by our commitment, but these alone will not create success or a sustainable business. Power comes from knowing that we cannot do things alone and by building trust and encouraging failure and one of the most vital parts to business is knowing your numbers. Without holistic vision in business, you are running blind. No matter what you hear, no business can succeed without you knowing your numbers and the impact your choices make in business, so give yourself permission to be shown how numbers can make sense rather than relying on what you have done in the past.

Understanding numbers doesn't need to be complicated, and once shown, you will never look back because when you understand the reason why you make the choices that you do, you will be able to better decide if you will keep something or make changes.

I will share that the number of people I know that say, 'Cathy, numbers aren't my thing,' is in excess of 90%, but that is only because they had not been shown how easy it can be. This small investment of your time in better understanding the numbers in your business will prevent you from being a statistic and will also enable you to make better choices.

Diversity in Life is Equally Important in Business

As you begin your journey forward and take control of the power that you hold within you, you will begin to take risks and do things differently. This is about giving yourself permission to be challenged, to be inclusive and to be diverse, just as much as it is to be innovative and to grow. It is through this combination that we discover new opportunities, and whilst there may be some failings, we want to celebrate them and take away the learnings as they will enable us to be one step closer to where we want to be.

Failing is an opportunity to do something different and is the beginning of giving others permission to do the same. So, if we are to be true in asking for diversity, we can also be true in showing others how to be diverse by taking risks, being different and stepping out to be seen for the choices that we take.

Doubt, hesitation or even fear is not who we are as women, and when we collaborate and are prepared to elevate those around us, we create diversity and acceptance of differences.

Investing in You

As you have read this chapter, if anything resonated with you, ask yourself how much you are prepared to invest in what you are doing and then ask if you have considered what or who you are excluding. This is your opportunity to invest in you.

Diversity is about your mind, your actions and how you perceive the impact you want to make in this world and who you choose to serve. Today is a new beginning, so step forward and create the path you choose to walk.

Here are my questions to you: What would you rather have? An ending you didn't want or a beginning you had not previously considered?

Five takeaway tips

1. Diversity is about including those that will challenge us in life.
2. 'Differences' include the celebration of failing and the choices we make to include them as part of the road map that we have created.
3. Knowing the impact you want to make is not about a service or a product, it is more than that.
4. Knowledge is not a destination. The more we know, the more we understand that there is more to learn.
5. Ask for help; nobody ever does anything alone. A shared journey is about elevating those around you.

Cathy Dimarchos

Cathy Dimarchos is known as an alchemist in business.

As the founder of Solutions2You, she is recognised as an unstoppable global award-winning business advisor and mentor to influential people. She is a humanitarian, two-time TEDX speaker and award-winning author who is future focused and works from her place of genius to create impact that elevates conscious leadership and supports others to think big. Her legacy is to create global impact that elevates humanity consciously.

With more than three decades of experience in finance and scaling businesses as well as being a qualified counsellor, Cathy is highly sought after all over the world as a professional advisor and motivational voice. She dedicates her time to sharing knowledge that combines people, business and situational skills to deliver tangible tools and skills so leaders can thrive and accelerate growth.

Her values take centrestage and business becomes honest and expressive as she helps people be comfortable with being uncomfortable, unlearn patterns that don't serve them and helps them step forward with clarity that will enable them to reach their goals.

With empathy and strategic positioning, she empowers people to establish healthy professional boundaries, to think limitlessly and to challenge norms, whilst rediscovering a curiosity of knowledge and themselves.

Cathy also holds AFSL licenses in the finance sector as a responsible manager for wholesale funds management. She understands compliance, budgets, risks and makes every transformation look easy.

Her book *Same People, Different Vision* is an Amazon number-one bestseller and was awarded the gold prize in MMH Pres book awards for business and leadership. It is filled with tips and tools for leaders of all ages so that they can shape a better tomorrow. Cathy has co-authored three other books focusing on female leadership. Those being number-one Amazon bestseller and bronze in the MMH Press awards, *Going against the Grain* – showcasing eight women across the globe who dared to dream differently and succeed, *The Women Changing the World* and *Unlock your Feminessence Code.*

Website: solutions2you.com.au
FB: facebook.com/CathyDimarchosCoachSpeaker
Instagram: instagram.com/solutions2you_consulting
Linkedin: linkedin.com/company/solutions2you-pty-ltd
Linkedin Personal: linkedin.com/in/cathy-dimarchos-advisor-and-mentor-to-ceos-and-executives-0218a090/?trk=public_profile_browsemap&originalSubdomain=au

The Role of Diversity in the Digital Era

The Impact of Women in Deep Tech

Dr Ingrid Vasiliu-Felltes

Global Landscape

The pandemic has been a massive catalyst for the digital era. Novel technologies are major drivers of change as they shape our society and economy at maximum velocity. Blending of the boundaries between physical and digital will likely continue with the increased adoption and rapid deployment of these novel technologies. Some of these, such as 5G, IoT, AI, blockchain, quantum or edge computing have a major disruptive potential globally.

Before the onset of this global pandemic, experts were already predicting an exponential adoption of digital technologies and they were encouraging businesses across all industries to engage in the digital transformation journey. With the dramatic world-wide economic and workforce changes we have been experiencing as a consequence of this pandemic, the predicted time line for completing the business transformation journey has markedly accelerated and it has now become an imperative for companies to start or accelerate their digital transformation process to adapt to the highly volatile geopolitical and economic environment of the post-pandemic digital era. Women have been disproportionately affected during the pandemic, and the gender divide has only widened for a variety of indicators across all industries. According to several reports published by United Nations, the World Health Organization, the World Bank, OECD and UNICEF, we have lost several decades of progress to attain the UN SDG 2030 agenda and SDG 5 has been markedly affected.

Even during favourable economic times, the road to a successful digital transformation is filled with hurdles and challenges, requiring a comprehensive strategy and disciplined deployment. Given the financial pressures and disruption in business operations due to the pandemic, it is now even more difficult for companies to design, deploy and complete all the stages required in a successful digital transformation process. Embedding diversity into the enterprise strategy has often been forgotten, neglected, avoided, underestimated or was only part of a public relations campaign. The new digital era heralds a major shift with novel mandates, increased societal expectations, heightened ESG consciousness and a generation that values purpose, diversity, equity and inclusion more than ever before. Women represent 49% of the world's population and must become an integral part of reshaping, recalibrating and reconfiguring the global business ecosystem.

To start this complex journey, organisations would need to complete a careful ESG and DEI risk analysis to understand what has changed, what new stakeholders have emerged and what new forces have a profound disruptive potential. More importantly, they need to understand the new values that drive their customer base and design customised metrics to monitor their performance in this new ecosystem. Harmonising their business, digital, ESG and DEI strategies is essential in ensuring long-term sustainability.

These unprecedented times call for innovative solutions and a revised approach to manage this volatile post-pandemic global business environment and to adapt to major emerging technology mega-trends. A state-of-the-art strategic road map and a carefully planned implementation strategy will be crucial, as well as adopting an ESG- and DEI-centric approach. There are several methods to accomplish this, however, the application of design thinking principles seems uniquely suited for a volatile and complex post-pandemic ecosystem. As stated, design thinking is only one option in the armamentarium available to business leaders. Adopting an abundance mindset and exponential thinking will also ensure diversity and inclusion for all business ecosystem domains.

Global surveys also indicate a key role for deep-tech solutions that combine AI, blockchain, IoT, advanced computing or even quantum technology and yield novel powerful platforms that aim to solve major pain points across various industries.

Women's role in this new technology-powered global ecosystem is essential, decision-makers must engage in a global collaborative effort to ensure that all facets are addressed for UN SDG 5 goals to be attained or even exceeded.

UN SDG 5 and the Global Economy – a Focus on AI, Blockchain and Quantum

The statistics of women in technology are staggering. Despite massive progress over the last few decades, the overall number of women employed in tech companies is still low. For example, the proportion of females in the United States in the top five technology companies reveals only about a quarter for each of the major technology giants like Google – 23%, Apple – 23%, Facebook – 23% or Microsoft – 20%. In engineering the numbers are even lower with only 20% of employees identified as female. The entrepreneurship ecosystem leadership role stats also leave a lot of room for improvement as only 37% of tech startups currently have a woman on their board.

A recent Goldman Sachs report emphasised why gender diversity can optimise productivity and enhance enterprise ROI. Additionally, companies with women on their boards are also performing better on their ESG-impact metrics. An HBR study on a small sample that will need to be replicated on a larger sample, found that a 10% increase in the ratio of women to men in the workforce correlated with a 7% increase in the market value for the company.

Women's Role in AI

Artificial intelligence has been a dominant player in the top digital technology trends shaping our global economy and society. The enterprise AI market report published recently highlights a total valuation of $9,880.4 million by 2023 with an impressive CAGR of 51.1%. Digital giants spent billions of dollars on R&D and acquisitions over the last four years with machine learning receiving the largest share. The OECD suggests that the internet, digital platforms, mobiles and digital financial services offer 'leapfrogging' opportunities that give women new possibilities to earn income, increase employment and access knowledge and general information. The changing skills requirements in the labour market – the same report emphasised the effects of AI on women entering the labor force – and the impacts of AI on women's work environment and career progression. Another recent Deloitte report also called attention to the fact that in 2020 women represented roughly 47% of the US labour force despite the fact that they receive the majority of graduate certificates, master's degrees and doctoral degrees from US institutions. A 2020 World Economic Forum report, however, found that women make up only 26% of data and AI positions in the workforce, while the Stanford Institute for Human-Centered AIs 2021 *AI Index Report* found that women make up just 16% of tenure-track faculty focused on AI globally.

Women's Role in Blockchain

Technology has witnessed exponential growth over the past few years and an unprecedented adoption rate globally triggered by the current pandemic. It has the potential to be a conduit for economic development and have a long-lasting impact from a societal and environmental perspective. The total market size is expected to reach a valuation of $176 billion by 2025 and $3.1 trillion by 2030 with a CAGR at or above 70% with slight variations depending on the domain (finance, retail, supply chain, etc.). The last two years have made a tremendous difference in propelling women into leadership roles in blockchain technology powered companies. With the transition to web 3.0, we expect this trend.

Women's Role in Quantum

The global quantum technology market size is currently valued at $487.4 million and is projected to reach $5 billion by 2028 and grow at a CAGR of 14.1%. As highlighted by a recent Harvard article we are witnessing a quantum adoption trend that is likely to accelerate adoption and possibly bridge the divide from research to the business ecosystem. Goldman Sachs, to Honeywell, Accenture, Rigetti, Google, Toshiba, Hewlett Packard, Microsoft, Fujitsu, Siemens and others are key players racing to attain market share or gain supremacy. The commercial applications keep increasing and therefore its business value, such as chemical and biological engineering, space defense and travel, fintech, life sciences, industrial manufacturing and global supply chain are a few examples where quantum computing proves superior to all other methods and has filed increased investments. Women have a unique opportunity to get in front of the curve for the upcoming large-scale adoption of quantum. This can be accomplished by designing and deploying robust education and talent management programs, incubators, accelerators and customised leadership programs.

Challenges

While great progress has been made, the gender gap remains significant and is estimated at $172 trillion – nearly two times the world's annual GDP, as stated by Mari Pangestu, World Bank Managing Director of Development Policy and Partnerships. Several international organisations highlight that women were hit harder on every level during the pandemic, the need to fundamentally rethink diversity and inclusion in the world of work and redesign the methodology of assigning board roles.

The board positions held by women as published in 2022 have increased from 24% to 29% at North American and European companies according to Moody's Investors Service. Deloitte also highlighted a clear correlation between women in top leadership roles and women in the boardroom. It also showcased that the most diverse boards tend to be found at companies with women chief executive officers or chairs. Interestingly, companies with women CEOs have significantly more balanced boards than those run by men – 33.5% women versus 19.4%. The statistics are similar for companies with a board chairwoman.

Solutions

Ethical leadership, skills of the future and impact investing are a powerful trifecta that can address some of the challenges.

Ethical leadership

Women leaders that wish to succeed in this highly virtualised, digitalised and hyperconnected environment will be required to display a complex armamentarium of novel skills, such as digital literacy and fluency, global citizenship, and mastery of applied ethics. Women leaders can establish themselves as ethical leaders in this digital era and play an active role in developing new laws, regulatory guidelines and frameworks that address the current lack of ESG- and EDI-consciousness in governments, board rooms or C-suites.

Skills of the future

Experts forecast a massive change in the jobs landscape triggered by a high degree of automation, digitisation, hyperconnectivity, remote work, etc. In this automation age the jobs ecosystem will be highly dynamic and volatile. Industries that employ primarily women will experience a high degree of job losses, upskilling and reskilling of the workforce to adapt to the new demands. Globally, 40 million to 160 million women may need to transition between occupations by 2030, often into higher-skilled roles according to WEF. The same report highlights important statistics such as: service oriented and clerical support occupations could account for 52% of women's job losses, and worldwide, 40 million to 160 million women – 7% to 24% of those currently employed – may need to transition across occupations.

However, new jobs will appear, and it is imperative to prepare young girls through novel education programs and young women through new career pathways for these new opportunities.

Women are poised to succeed in the new digital era if they improve their digital literacy, digital fluency and computational thinking, deploy their emotional and social intelligence, as well as their creative and innovative mindset which are all top-ranked skills for 2030. Work-from-home facilitator to fitness commitment counsellor and algorithm bias auditor to cyber calamity forecaster, are all novel jobs predicted for 2030.

Key decision-makers will need to create supportive programs that allow women to capitalise on education, career and skills training opportunities. High priorities include more investment in the provision of child care, safe and affordable transportation, addressing stereotypes about occupations, boosting women's access to mobile internet and digital skills in emerging economies and supporting women in STEM professions and entrepreneurship.

Impact investing

A 2022 study by BNY calculated that if women invested at the same rate as men, there could be more than $3.22 trillion of additional capital to invest globally with over $1.87 trillion flowing into more responsible investing, the nascent field of gender-lens investing.

Women's mission is to achieve a world in which all women and girls can exercise their basic human rights and can unlock their full economic and social potential. Achieving gender equality is at the heart of achieving the sustainable development goals and requires strong public–private partnerships that will direct greater flows of financing toward gender equality objectives.

Based on Ernst and Young's research, 67% of female investors globally stated that their wealth managers misunderstood their goals. This dissatisfaction is also demonstrated by the finding that 70% of women switch their wealth relationship to a new financial institution within a year of their spouse's death.

Based on research from Fidelity in 2021, the number of women in the US who say they are more interested in investing has risen by 50% since the start of the pandemic. 67% of women respondents were investing outside their retirement plans, compared to only 44% in 2018, which is consistent with other statistics captured during the pandemic. Furthermore, UBS's 2021 Investor Pulse survey highlighted that while 68% of women now felt more comfortable talking about finances, there is still an execution gap. Another positive trend identified that financial participation has also increased among married women. A 2020 McKinsey report showed that 30% more married women were making financial and investment decisions than five years previously.

Future Directions

We are on the cusp of the next IR and women are an integral part of the transition from the fourth to the fifth, as they represent the majority workforce in several domains such as education, health care and social work.

With the transition toward the next generation internet called web 3.0 and the birth of a new digital economy powered by converging deep tech, women have a unique opportunity to turn a crisis into an opportunity. The creator economy, social entrepreneurship and gig economy can be powerful catalysts for future generations of women that are well prepared and empowered to take full advantage of this new era.

By designing novel education systems, novel business models, novel financial instruments and novel talent management solutions that reduce the gender divide we can change the existing paradigm by offering future generations a more inclusive, diverse and equitable global business and entrepreneurship ecosystem.

References

- weforum.org/agenda/2022/03/women-work-break-the-mould
- unwomen.org/en/news-stories/press-release/2022/05/blackrock-and-un-women-to-promote-gender-lens-investing
- wp.oecd.ai/app/uploads/2022/03/The-Effects-of-AI-on-the-Working-Lives-of-Women.pdf
- worldbank.org/en/news/press-release/2022/03/01/nearly-2-4-billion-women-globally-don-t-have-same-economic-rights-as-men
- www2.deloitte.com/us/en/insights/industry/technology/technology-media-and-telecom-predictions/2022/statistics-show-women-in-technology-are-facing-new-headwinds.html
- mckinsey.com/~/media/mckinsey/featured%20insights/gender%20equality/the%20future%20of%20women%20at%20work%20transitions%20in%20the%20age%20of%20automation/mgi-the-future-of-women-at-work-exec-summary-july-2019.pdfhttps://www.ubs.com/global/en/wealth-management/insights/chief-investment-office/market-insights/2022/women-and-investing-reimagining-wealth-advice.html#:~:text=A%202022%20study%20by%20BNY,flowing%20into%20more%20responsible%20investing
- www2.deloitte.com/us/en/pages/consulting/articles/state-of-women-in-ai-today.html

Dr Ingrid Vasiliu-Feltes

Expert advisor to the European Union Blockchain Observatory Forum, senior senator and secretary-general of the science, technology and innovation committee, secretary-general research institute, as well as USA country director for the World Business Angel Investment Forum (WBAF) – an affiliated partner of the G20 Global Partnership for Financial Inclusion (GPFI) chaired by the Queen Maxima of the Netherlands, CEO of Softhread Inc., board member and chief innovation officer Government Blockchain Association, board member of The Partners In Digital Health Institute, the founder and CEO of the Institute for Science, Entrepreneurship and Investments. Recipient of numerous awards, most notably the WBAF World Excellence Award for Social Entrepreneurship 2021, the Top 100 Visionary In Education Award 2021, the Top 100 Global Women in Leadership Award

2021, the Top 100 World Women Vision Award for Innovation and Technology in 2021, the Top 100 Healthcare Leader 2020 Award, Top 100 Finance Leader 2020 Award. Named Top 25 Quantum Technology Leader, Ranked 2 Global Leader in Digital Twins Technologies, Top 50 Global Leader in Health, Top 150 Women in Business To Follow. Forbes Business Council member, co-founder of the WBAF World Smart Cities Economic Development Commission and global thought leader on digital advocacy, digital ethics, digital transformation, contributing to numerous UN SDG 2030 global initiatives. Author of several books and teaching at the University of Miami Business School, Executive MBA Program and at the WBAF Business School.

Chronicles of a Migrant Woman in Business

Hilda Julian Johani

Acknowledgements

To my children, Kuzi, Casey and Caellan, and my mom Stella. Thank you for being the constant element in my life and always being there.

Introduction

I'm not Black, I am Brown. Why am I constantly referred to as Black? In contrast, the colour black and brown is different. Look at me closer. What do you see? Am I Black? Or am I Brown?

I am a Brown migrant woman in business. I've been through a divorce. I'm a proud mom of three biological children that I have raised alone for the more significant part of their lives. At the same time, I am called to be a mother to many in the community. I am a diverse woman. I sentimentally liken myself to the woman in Proverbs 31. I'm blessed, and I'm highly favoured. I'll share some highlights of my life and moments of tears along my journey. This humble beginning has provided me with the building blocks that are still helping me structure the global business empire of my heart's desire.

Let's share my chronicles as I celebrate my diversity.

My story begins now.

Goodbye Past, Hello Future

On 12 February 2002, I arrived at Birmingham International Airport from Zimbabwe. I'd been through tremendous emotional trauma in my life. My parents and I unanimously agreed that having gone through what I went through, perhaps it would be a good idea to take time out and visit the United Kingdom, have a pause, as I could certainly afford it – and maybe find myself, so to speak. My thoughts ran towards my little girl; what could separate me from her? She was only two years old at the time in 2001. So, I decided to wait until she was three years old to leave for the United Kingdom, as I never wanted her to forget me. So, a year later, on the night of 10 February 2002, I waited until she had gone to bed, as I could not look her in the eye to say goodbye. I took her in my arms while she slept and cried so much. I prayed for her and blessed her. I never knew that it would not be until 3 March 2004 that I would see her again.

Why Birmingham?

As you would have it, I picked Birmingham right off the map in my depressed state. I remember simply looking at the map, and there was Birmingham! And I said to myself, *Right! So how do I get there?* I had all the flights from Harare to Johannesburg, Johannesburg to Paris and Paris to Birmingham. I remember coming out of the airport and sitting outside – *Now what?* I had it all planned to stay at a hotel in Leamington Spa for two weeks, and that's what I did! That's when it all started. I came with such a focus because I had gone through such a significant separation and devastation. That was my push factor. I had my daughter on my mind, and that was my main driver. Within two weeks, I was volunteering around Birmingham and got myself enrolled in a college while working twenty hours a week. Every penny I earned, I would send back home.

The Struggle for Recognition

Being a migrant Brown woman was not easy. I was met with prejudice about my skin colour, the fact that I was an African, and the political relationship between Zimbabwe and the UK at the time did not help my situation. I was born in Zimbabwe and did all of my accountancy training there. I gained professional accountancy experience. The educational system was similar to other existing methods. Despite this similarity –we were even using the same textbooks – my accounting qualifications were not recognised or accepted in the new country! I was already educated, experienced and had a good command of the Queen's English, but no-one seemed interested in all that at the time. Time and time again, I was overlooked in job roles and never had any chances. For one reason or the other, I didn't get the job. I can particularly recall working for a central accounting agency, the only one that had at that time recognised that I had professional accounting qualifications and experience from one of the top four accounting firms in the world. I had passed all their competency assessments with flying colors. They placed me in a particular role with a company in Digbeth in Birmingham. The task was to put in order an accounting department that was simply a dumping hole for used documents! No-one was available to sort this mess.

I arrived at my assignment with my usual smart suit attire,

and people in the office exchanged glances, as in my opinion, people didn't make an effort to dress up for work. In my last role in Zimbabwe, we even had an annual clothing allowance to ensure we looked at the part for our roles! This realisation was a paradigm shift in what was the norm for me.

I was working with a young eighteen-year-old girl who had just left college and was starting to find her way. We got to know each other, and sharing my career experience and zeal to train and teach with her, she decided to follow my lead on this project. I was familiar with accounting documentation, so we quickly completed this task over eight weeks. During this task, I felt excluded in the office, apart from my young workmate. If I entered the room, they would stop laughing or chatting or look down at their tasks. I would walk into the office and say good morning, and no-one would answer. I remember frequently catching the line manager giving me a resentful look every time he walked past me. We completed the task, and acknowledgments and thanks were made not to me but to my young colleague, whom they presumed had pioneered the way. That night, I got a call from the agency who advised me that the company did not need me anymore. The familiar story of the gut feeling of exclusion ripped through me. I asked myself why I was excluded. I had worked for multiple agencies within two years, as most jobs just stopped and started. Through these experiences, I began using my break times to develop myself by reading motivation and business books. I invested in short business startup courses and pieces of training in-between jobs, as self-development is one of my key strengths.

I left Zimbabwe as a part-qualified accountant, but I had the experience of working in a professional firm and for large international companies. I also started doing accounting books for small businesses at an early age. Coming to the UK, I was frustrated when I kept getting lowly jobs that I was more than qualified for and didn't even require any qualifications. Looking back over the years, I realised that I was learning systems and processes – things that would be necessary to support the client bases I invest in in my businesses now. I understand procedures – I know back-office methods and what goes on behind the scenes in many companies. So, this now makes me a more effective business consultant, as I have more hands-on experience.

I worked as a carer for many years, even during times when health and safety were not prioritised for caregivers, and I suffered some injuries that at the time there was no compensation for. I'm writing my story to encourage someone out there and to say, 'Hey, you! I am CEO of HBBA Care in England now and Kavaclan Care in Northern Ireland, but I was once a carer too.'

'Never judge me by what you see, but get to know me first.'
– Hilda Johani, CMA.

Hilda Johani, CMA

I'm a certified management accountant by profession and have written close to fifty exams in this discipline in my lifetime. I am proud to accredit the beginning of my career to my dad, the late Dominic Johani, who directed me and inspired me to take on this profession as he was an accountant himself. In my anthology section 'cost leadership and the hustle', I go deeper into this side of my business and other technical know-how about finances – a topic I believe every budding entrepreneur or businessperson should come to terms with and understand.

I arrived in the UK at the age of twenty-eight, and despite the career hiccups along the way, I still desired to be somebody in this profession. I wanted to run my own business more seriously in the UK, as I was doing people's books in the early years of my career. Going back to the thread of jobs I was working, such as cleaning, care work and factory work, I still desired to run an accountancy business even then. Going back to my experience working in a professional accounting environment, I heard the words spoken in my life in 2003: 'Stop waiting for people to give you a job and promote you. Start your own business. Employ yourself and employ others!' And that's what I did and started laying the foundations for that.

I enrolled in university and did my Bachelor of Accounting and Finance – and the first year was a breeze through because I had done the work and being in the uni class was a revision for me. As mentioned earlier, my accounting qualifications from my home country were not recognised, so I was willing to do the work from scratch to get myself qualifications that would be accepted. I had time on my hands, and that's when I started my business. I got married in 2004, and thanks to that marriage of ten years, despite being divorced now, my status changed and I was now able to have more opportunities without limiting my immigration status. At last, my little girl, now aged five, finally came to join me in the UK. She too began her school life with me.

The business idea was birthed out of my reasoning that, with two kids now, I needed something that was going to give me both a job and allow me to study, and the solution was that I had to start my own business as I needed something that I could control. I would juggle university, my small bookkeeping business and school runs!

In terms of getting first clients, which probably a lot of young people do not realise, it is about positioning yourself. I came across an advert that required a bookkeeper for a dance group. I had to volunteer! Now, I certainly cannot dance – but I thought to put a group together, put my name forward for the bookkeeper role and coordinate them to dance! The position was voluntary work, and I loved it! I was soon able to take on another client and I started growing my portfolio that way. What began as Hilda Burke Bookkeeping & Accounting (HBBA) is what has evolved now to HBBA Certified Management Accountants.

'When you lean in and get into the game, other opportunities will open up.'
– Hilda Johani, CMA

Accounting, Training, Then Care

Doing my qualification twice was not bad because it opened up more significant opportunities for me. At university, I met two extraordinary young ladies, both eighteen years old. I was thirty-seven years old at the time. These young ladies had observed that I was always in a mad rush after classes and wanted to know why. I then told them it was because I had a business! They got interested and started working with me, from literally year one through to year three. Through this I saw the value of people getting work experience early in life and being able to bounce off their careers faster. I decided to develop an accounting work experience program. By the time we all graduated, I had trained seventy-five accounting graduates, and I had even gotten a grant to do that! These were my classmates and I had helped equip them for jobs.

I discovered that my passion for teaching and training grew. How that happened was that through the roles I had worked as an accountant, I was always the 'Nelly' in the office. Sit with Nelly if you want something shown – Hilda will show you! So, I was always the person to show others the ropes. An opportunity to start teaching A-Level accountants arose through some business colleagues in my building. This was the benchmark for me to do a teaching qualification. I enrolled in a postgraduate degree in Education Certificate at Birmingham City University in 2012, and I was teaching accounting. I began to teach AAT accounting and set up colleges for clients, birthing the idea of starting my own training business.

I have always had time to mentor and teach other people. I never knew potentially, one day, I would be the owner of HBBA Training Academy LTD. HBBA Training Academy is an accredited training provider delivering courses in health and social care. Further, I write and produce my training programs over and above the available mandatory training. I provide a four-week business startup program in the health care sector, 'Care & Supported Living Start-Up Course', helping people to start up the right way more cost-effectively, avoiding losses and hitting brick walls. I provide mentoring, support and resources for individuals to help them get started in this business. At the end of the four weeks, I expect to see the birthing of a viable company registered, a bank account opened and clients having the tools to obtain their first contract.

The vision now for the training company is to work towards accreditation for the accounting qualification, starting with a program for Level 2 AAT students, exposing them to mentorship and work experience opportunities. This vision comes from the realisation that box-standard qualifications do not suit business requirements in the market because schools and colleges are producing academics. Still, work-based training would combine that and bring the theory and the practical aspect together and gel the two.

Meanwhile, in the accounting business, I set up many people

who were starting health care businesses and I observed that in only six months they were doing better than me! That's when I decided to get into health care and birthed HBBA Care LTD in 2015. HBBA Care has now become our core business, providing services for young adults and children with learning difficulties. Besides being the flagship of HBBA Group, this care business is what has brought me more personal gratification than any of the other division. I love what I do! I have a very hands-on approach to this business and love providing personal care to these vulnerable groups. If I achieve the outcome of helping them get out of bed, making their beds, their breakfast and putting on their clothes the right way, I get all the personal fulfilment and gratification. I have a team of carers who assist and live with them daily. We have meetings, do things together and get involved with the families. I remain very engaged with them because I want to know each person on the ground, and they make a difference in my life.

My accounting apprentices and my highflyers are the ones I have left to be hands-on in the office running the accountancy business. I supervise and mentor. I am getting it all!

'Do not despise your humble beginnings, but nurture them, as one day they will be multiplied.'
– Hilda Johani, CMA

hildajohani.com

With my accounting business, which is now known as HBBA Certified Accountants, HBBA Training Academy Ltd and HBBA Care Ltd, it was then that I met a game changer, Hazel Herrington, of Herrington Worldwide Publications. Hazel began working with me and my brand hildajohani.com, blending all my business concepts and ideas to provide business mentoring and startup support. She invited me to speak at a phenomenal platform, Lady America's Power: Barriers & Bias – The Status of Women in Leadership event in November 2021. We are still on that journey.

If I backtrack into my high school years in Zimbabwe, we were taught public speaking. For all my years in high school I won competitions for public speaking, so I have always had the gift of the gab. Now, because I have been running many different things in my career, I did not quite understand who I was until the concept of an entrepreneur hit home and I realised that's what I must be – an entrepreneur. I had always felt I was riding on three horses; no matter how much you can control them, it isn't easy. With the light-bulb moment of realising I was an entrepreneur, I decided to bring everything under one roof and brand myself – hildajohani.com – as all my offering is at the back of many different qualifications and experiences. As I sit with a client to give business advice, work on their books, provide coaching, mentoring and change management, I anticipate that one can see the holistic make-up of where I have come from and where I am going.

The brand officially launched on 4 December 2021, at a celebration night event held at the Belfrey Restaurant and Resort, Birmingham. It was the night of Thanksgiving. We witnessed a coming together of all HBBA stakeholders made up of accounting, training academy, the people we look after in care and our staff team, to a black-tie dining experience that was genuinely electric and beyond even my expectations. I want to do this again and again, as my thanks to all our stakeholders will never stop.

Keeping It Real and Not Giving Up

Looking back now to that young Hilda that just picked Birmingham off the map, I am grateful that the past twenty years have come together for my family and me in this way.

I am thankful for my journey. The early years of separation from my daughter were hard. I did not hold her in my arms for two and a half years. I used to cry as I thought about how she grew up without me. Upon reuniting, we had to go through the hurdles of overcoming the effect of that separation. We had to heal and overcome the fear of separation. I can relate to all other immigrant women who have had to part with loved ones, albeit for a short time, to pursue a better life for everyone. My daughter is twenty-three years old now, and we are very close when writing this. As much as I have expanded on the business platform, I could not have done it without her! She is there to encourage me, and in the times I have felt like giving up and packing it in, she is the one that has always been there to get me to focus and appreciate the foundation of all this.

The ten years of my marriage were not easy. I was ambitious. I was aspiring to do better for my life and children. But, as it takes two to tango, there wasn't always the same piece of music playing. I became depressed and overweight, and for many years I had very low self-esteem and could not see any light at the end of the tunnel. As we were in church, the concept of divorce had a stigma attached to it, and further, the counselling and support available through the church were somehow discouraging and it was just till death do us part. It was suffocating, and I was unhappy. I eventually decided to get out. And now, a few years later, I am grateful that it did turn out for good and we are both living much-fulfilled lives.

I am grateful for my other two children, an eighteen-year-old son and my seven-year-old youngest son. They are pillars of unbelievable support and my greatest cheerleaders.

Having gone through such an ordeal, and I'm sure many people can relate to something like this, I drowned myself in my business, and later, opportunities came that I was able to form my care business, HBBA Care LTD. The establishment and growth of my care business has given me wings. My experience in this sector has not only helped me establish my own business, but is another tool that demonstrates my entrepreneurial ability. I have emerged as a well-respected business consultant that gives more added value to my clients due to my diverse wealth of experience in various business environments.

There have been wolves in sheep's clothing along my journey, but somehow you begin to understand people more and who they are not.

They say my race will only get me so far, but I will keep going and reach the destiny I can bear.

I never listened to those voices! Instead, I've focused on the hills where my help comes from.

'People will try to discourage you from pursuing your dreams. Don't listen. You are you, and they are them.'
– Hilda Johani, CMA

Hilda Julian Johani

Hilda Johani is a self–made entrepreneur who started her early business life, in Birmingham UK, with the establishment of an Accountancy Business in 2007. HBBA Certified Management Accountants continues to support business with Statutory Financial Accounting Reporting. In 2015, Hilda then branched into the Healthcare sector to establish HBBA Care, which is achieving outcomes of supporting Young Adults with Learning Difficulties in the community. Due to a passion for teaching and training, in 2016, Hilda established HBBA Training Academy, which focuses on Work-Based Training and delivery of high-er-level qualifications in the Health & Social Care sector. HBBA Training Academy will be delivering Accounting Qualifications (AAT) soon. Hilda Johani prides herself as a seasoned Business Consultant, Financial & Accounting Expert, and Speaker, drawing from experience gained throughout her career. Hilda is a proud mother of a daughter and two young men aged: 23,17 & 6 years old.

When the Why is Clear, the How Is Easy

Joanna James

Why – the three most powerful letters in existence. By asking this simple question we find purpose and meaning in everything ...

It was 11:45pm as I sat up in bed, the room was chilly, the pillows smelled of lavender and they supported my back well. I pondered the day just passed and the future ahead, I knew I had to gain clarity before the clock ticked past midnight, why?

It was my fiftieth birthday and naturally a point of deep reflection on the first half-century of my lifetime.

I had been joined earlier in the day by several lifelong girl-friends, and as we laughed about how nothing had really changed, I realised somehow, for me, everything had. I found myself asking why it was that a group of such intelligent capable women were all, in different ways, struggling. How could it be that my friends were now comparing the cost of a cucumber at two different supermarkets on a weekly basis – why?

'You still have so much energy for life …'

'Well, of course I do, I am just getting started,' I said. As the smiles and giggles faded, I began to wonder, *Am I really different somehow?* Around 11:55 my takeaway from the day suddenly hit me. The first fifty years of my life I had spent doing what was right, what was expected of me, mostly looking after other people. The second half I'll be doing what really moves me, and please get out of my way, I've got things to do, I'm fifty!

In order to understand why diversity is the new way of doing business, we must first explore what 'diversity' is and the role it plays in the future of business, particularly for women.

I have long been a believer that a business is a co-creation of the people who work within it and reflects the values and beliefs of the owner/s and leaders of the business. If we are to truly affect change then the discussion starts here; diversity begins with the approach we bring to our own thinking.

Whilst many companies espouse to promote diversity, 'diversity' alone is not enough for a business to be progressive, it requires an element of inclusion and equity to really create meaningful change in the world. To simplify the seduction of falling prey to buzzwords, let's take a moment to examine what each of these terms means.

Diversity can be described simply as the presence of difference. This is usually evaluated by people in a business, however, it could also extend to the products or services a company offers.

Inclusion can be described as persons of different identities being accepted, valued and appreciated within business. However, this may also extend to customers and the external people a business serves.

Equity is an approach that ensures everyone has access to the same opportunities. This may be considered by how businesses promote opportunity for its people, however, it may also extend to how a business creates more equity within the world.

It's fundamental that all conversations require context. Any discussion on diversity must begin with questioning the parameters of the conversation with a frank review of how the diversity relates to the context of inclusion and equity within a business. Not to do so simply fails to demonstrate any diversity of thinking.

Discussions about creating diversity for diversity's sake lack the evaluation of why diversity is important in the first place, or what type of diversity is required.

With a title like *Lady Diversity Power*, the obvious first level of consideration for diversification might be gender. I could talk forever on the importance of gender diversity, especially in business. With research confirming that organisations with more women in senior positions are more profitable, more socially responsible and provide safer, higher-quality customer experiences, one would think diversification through gender is a no-brainer in business. However, this can also bring forced quotas, superficial approaches to placing talent in positions and internal discord through a lack of inclusion generally. To understand the length of the path ahead, here are a few statistics that speak for themselves regarding the current state of businesses in Australia.

According to the Australian Workplace Gender Equality report, women comprise 47.9% of all employed persons in Australia. However, the full-time average weekly ordinary earnings for women are 13.8% less than for men. This culminates with most women entering retirement with on average one-third of the savings of men. Coupling this with women over forty-five becoming the fastest group of growing homelessness it is easy to see why this is an issue that needs to be addressed. If we look at the top structures of corporations, women hold 17.6% of chair positions and 31.2% of directorships and represent 19.4% of CEOs and 34.5% of key management personnel. Given that 51% of the population are women it's easy to see that businesses have a way to go to represent the sexes equally.

The discussion around equality for women as a part of providing diversity in companies cannot be separated from the need for inclusion of more women in senior positions. The drive for inclusion within businesses requires a frank discussion about the importance of equity within a business. This is what will ultimately drive an increase in equity externally in the world.

As we continue to explore the importance of diversity it would be remiss when considering gender not to acknowledge that according to *Medical News Today*, there are seventy-two genders, so in fact, a discussion on gender is a far wider topic than just male and female representation.

If we look then to further diversity through the inclusion of various nationalities, we embark on another layer of opportunity. Currently there are 197 countries in the world – well, countries that are officially recognised, anyway. Perhaps businesses can grow diversity through a wider inclusion of persons from differing nationalities?

Given the rise of new global employment via outsourcing, this change in business is already growing as many companies develop teams around the world.

According to NTT Services, 45% of companies have planned to increase their outsourcing since the pandemic, often focusing on finding skill sets they can't access in-house. Whilst 24% of small companies say they outsource to increase efficiency levels, many small businesses also use outsourcing to access specialist skills not readily available in the local marketplace.

However, the elephant in the room is that the number one

reason for outsourcing for 70% of companies is cost reduction, as outsourcing lowers the costs associated with hiring in-house staff.

Unfortunately, the intent for this type of diversification is primarily driven by cost savings, not the general desire to expand a more inclusive work environment. And it certainly isn't representative of equity when we consider the pay and position inequality that this typically creates. This diversification driven by monetary requirements often leads business into a culturally challenging space and if not managed adeptly can create an us-and-them divide, resulting in the opposite of inclusion.

To further expand upon this complexity is the variety of ethnic groups within these countries. According to the 'Ethnic Groups Worldwide' study there are over 650 ethnic groups in the world and an even more staggering statistic is that there are over 7,000 languages spoken in the world, resulting in permutations of heritage as well as spoken dialect and communication. To expect that smaller companies or the individuals within these businesses would have the capacity to effectively manage the operational complexities is naive at best.

To complete the tapestry of a true diversification, we would need to also create an inclusive environment for personal beliefs, faith and religion. The world currently has over 10,000 different religions, so if we start to look at the now compounded combination of diversity possibilities we can see that 2x72x197x650x7,000x10,000 is a factor of *129,074,400,000,000,000* possible ways we can diversify our businesses with any one person who joins a team.

'Ideals are like the stars: we never reach them, but like the mariners of the sea, we chart our course by them.' – Carl Schurz

Diversity for diversity's sake lacks an evaluation of why

diversity is important in the first place, leaving gaps when considering what type of diversity is required. We can see the possible benefits from diversity are enormous and so too are the potential challenges. So how do we navigate this topic and deliver meaningful positive change through diversity in business?

In my many years of growing a successful company, upon reflection, diversity falls into two main areas of demonstration: diversity of thinking and diversity of experience.

The categories of diversity reviewed above are simply subcategories of life that create various modes of thinking and experience to add for consideration. Remembering that to appreciate and integrate diversity most effectively we also need inclusion as well as equity otherwise the experience becomes a divergent one, pulling things apart.

'Those who can't change their minds can't change anything.'
– George Bernard Shaw

Diversity of Thinking

I recall in my younger years just how uncomfortable it was for me to be in a place where a vast difference of opinion was expressed. The many times I could cut the air thick with tension and that often deep sinking feeling of, *Oh no, so-and-so has really rocked the boat*. I often found myself playing the role of the peacekeeper, jumping in to bring a better understanding amongst the parties. Somehow it just felt uncomfortable when people couldn't understand each other. Often there were times when my enthusiasm to take the edge off resulted in the discordant energy being redirected in my direction. Like all energy in motion, who was I to alter the path of its expression, after all, it had a purpose to fulfil. It wasn't until well into my forties that I realised that diversity of opinion is entirely different to diversity of thinking.

As I progressed further with more and more responsibility in my career, I began to see that encouraging team discussions with various and different types of thinking was an asset to any situation the business was facing. Being able to look at a single issue from a variety of perspectives always resulted in a far better solution. Not only were the immediate outcomes more effective, they also had covered off more potential risks to be avoided.

Being an international company that insourced to the Philippines and Vietnam, our team was already diverse in many of the subcategories covered above. My role as a leader evolved to ask more and more questions – 'This is how I see things, what do you think?' became my new go-to question. I was always inquisitive and appreciative of the varying points of view.

This process of enquiry was always enhanced at our annual team strategy meetings, where we intentionally created a deep dive environment of synergy through variety in thinking. All preconceived ideas were left at the door and the executive team embarked on an immersive journey to create a new path forward. I began to see why Stephen Covey said, 'Strength lies in differences not in similarities.'

And then one day a very strange thing happened, I began to realise that I was learning to think about issues using different styles of thinking myself; diverse thinking was becoming a skill in itself. As this process progressed, I became less attached to my need for an opinion and more open to exploring various options using different styles of thinking, seeking better solutions. I noticed that some ways of thinking developed more easily than others and I still had to be conscious of my bias, assumptions and blind spots. I let go of my need to be right and sought the right result.

Whilst often confronting, I began to grow my thoughts.

Over the next few years, we embarked on creating an environment across the group that embraced difference, promoting appreciation of varied thinking across the business. This fostered an environment of participation across the team and new nonlinear ways of working began to appear. Leadership began to grow in an entirely different way as people's participation became less about hierarchy and more about collaboration and innovation.

I wasn't surprised that many years later I came across the research that there are, in fact, seven different styles of thinking: critical, analytical, creative, abstract, concrete, convergent and divergent. Being an experiential learner on a deeper level I knew this to be true.

Rather than doing a deep dive into each modality here, I'd rather use the time to ask why it had taken so many years to come across this learning and why as a skill it is not more actively taught in practicality for anyone participating in business? Whilst naturally we will all have innate ways of thinking, just like any skill, thinking can be learnt. If we are to embrace diversity as the new way of doing business, we must embrace the foundational practice to encourage diverse forms of thinking.

As a side note, once again, without the equity and inclusion of the people to participate with different thinking styles, this rich diversification would never have been possible within the business.

> *'Life is a succession of lessons which must be lived to be understood.'* – Ralph Waldo Emerson

Diversity of Experience

Having sat in countless interviews hiring people for the team, I have a rather different view on what experience actually means.

Obviously, a business will have a practical or technical expertise that they seek for a role, however, for me, I was always more interested in what was underneath, being the unique personal experience that a person would bring.

Typically, businesses appreciate a variety of applied professional experience, rarely do they rate what a depth of life experience will bring to the table too. As I began to become more and more focused on the soft skills of leadership – persuasion, negotiation, empathy, resilience, kindness and compassion – I realised that these are the very skills life brings to you. Understanding the whole of a person, seeing them for all of who they are, having them feel that they didn't need to hide away parts of themselves for fear of being rejected and judged.

For much of my own life I struggled, being a jill-of-all-trades and a master of none. I often questioned what was the true contribution that I was even making. I envied those around me who appeared to have clarity, had I somehow missed out on my specialty, my niche, my expertise? As all sudden insights do, it hit me one day – variety was my master skill, and this is exactly what I used every day to create a difference in the lives of others too.

How could it be that it was so blindly obvious and yet hidden from view, it was the diversity of life experience that was my superpower. The good, the bad, the ugly and everything in-between I was starting to collect all the separated parts of me and reclaim the woman I truly wanted to be. It was time to live the ultimate diversity and include all aspects of me equally, for the first time in a long time I felt authentic.

I wonder how different life might be if the world was run by businesses that supported this type of equity, a genuine authenticity for their people and the people that they serve. This may very well be the new way of doing business and just the change the world needs.

Perhaps my ideals are ahead of this current time, yet as I reflected upon lunch earlier that day, all I could see was the length and breadth and diversity of life experiences before me. Perhaps a different type of diversity, one that values the wisdom we gain with age, might create better opportunities for the future after all? If we have any hope of creating positive change we must begin to look at diversity in a completely different way. This will require a willingness to move beyond the surface layer of buzzwords and latest trends with a persistent dedication and consistent inquiry to asking – why?

'Find your why and you'll find your way.' – John C Maxwell

Joanna James

Joanna James is a successful business founder and chief ambassador for the successful woman. With a varied career, Joanna has a love of people, beautiful spaces, business and entrepreneurship.

As Australia's youngest dual-licensed architect and builder, she knows how to construct and build successful companies. Her contribution to the award-winning non-bank Mortgage Ezy business recognised her as principal of the year (WIFA 2020) as well as president of the MFAA Managers Forum. Continually redefining her leadership style, from humble beginnings of doing it all, the Ezy group now spans internationally.

Joanna's contributions are embodied in over forty national awards, including back-to-back BRW Fastest Growing Company three times, Best Home loans Money Magazine four times, Best Nonbank Australian Lending awards, recognition by MPA,

Advisor, MFAA and many others. At the core of this recognition is the consistent and steady business growth despite market conditions to now more than $1.5 billion of loans per year and a managed book over $4.5 billion.

Joanna is featured in *Entrepreneur, The Advisor, MPA, Australian Broker, CIO* and *Insights Success*. She speaks on topics ranging from resilience, self-confidence, mindset, leadership, business culture, entrepreneurship, success and of course her latest book *Mind Body Spaces.*

Joanna is also an award-winning architect and has been recognised for her sustainable design winning best overall and commercial fit out for her pegasus design. Her innovative bio-home in Byron Bay was also showcased on *I Own Australia's Best Home,* and was one of the first homes in Australia to fully incorporate the principles of building biology.

She believes that every woman deserves access to vital success information that is not taught in mainstream education. Today she empowers others to rise above limitations, sharing new ways of success learning for women so they may create change and freedom. Her mantra is anything is possible!

Revolutionising Education for Women Through Radicalisation of Curriculum

Dr Khomotso Mashalane

Education within marginalised groups of societies has and continues to serve as a cornerstone for the building, rebuilding or reconstructing of their systems. Meaning, what is taught in any community can establish new methods of practice, what is excluded (in teaching) in any community can re-establish problematic notions that may perpetuate backwards ways of living. It has been an undeniable fact that what we are taught – from households, to schools, to friendships, to politics, to workplaces – we internalise and we process as normal. This is the societal representation of a vicious cycle, a pendulum swing that launches from one side (sexist non-inclusive backward education) to the other side (continued lack of access for young children to radical education).

Any transformative community prioritises education, learner-ship and teaching, with the aim to acknowledge the imperative role that educating youths plays in empowering individuals as well as a grand scheme in society. We start by recognising the detrimental class-related gap between groups of society. The wealthy across all spectrums experience excellence in all its forms, while the less fortunate are excluded from what societies deem as the best.

To make a contribution to improving the condition of women, we need not only provide them with more education, jobs, and laws but also to reframe our understanding of gender in society. This means not losing sight of the fact that all gender asymmetries are connected through an ideology (with various degrees of intensity across societies).

Gender creates conditions that are advantageous for men in terms of political and economic leadership, but destructive in quality of life stemming from the messages and practices of violence and force linked to masculinity. Moreover, gender operates across all social classes.

The second task is to decide how to teach new material, a process that typically involves reconceptualising one's disciplines in light of a race, class, ultimately gender-based analysis. Often this means learning to move typically marginal groups into the core of the curriculum. Furthermore, efforts can be made to present issues. The third task is to structure classroom dynamics that ensure a safe atmosphere to support learning for *all the students*.

Individuality and difference in education, while connoting separation, are understood as openness and communication. Individuality is essentially engagement and connection. It must therefore transcend all forms of solipsism and discrimination. A realistic view of inclusive education engages man's context through his being simultaneously *separated* and *connected*. Diversity in education enriches the learners' environment and vice versa. What is saliently being highlighted here is the *identity*, or better, the *dignity* that underlies an individual person.

Promotion of inclusive education then happens in the open understanding and experiencing of the value and dignity of the person.

Gender Equality in Education

Gender-equitable education systems empower children and promote the development of life skills – like self-management, communication, negotiation and critical thinking – that young people need to succeed. They close skills gaps that perpetuate pay gaps and build prosperity for entire countries.

Gender-equitable education systems can contribute to reductions in school-related gender-based violence and harmful practices, including child marriage[1] and female genital mutilation[2].

Gender-equitable education systems help keep both girls and boys in school, building prosperity for entire countries.

An education free of negative gender norms has direct benefits for boys, too. In many countries, norms around masculinity can fuel disengagement from school, child labour, gang violence and recruitment into armed groups. The need or desire to earn an income also causes boys to drop out of secondary school, as many of them believe the curriculum is not relevant to work opportunities.

Ultimately what can be seen as an effective way to push change forward, is through implementing tangible methods of research.

---

1 unicef.org/protection/child-marriage
2 unicef.org/protection/female-genital-mutilation

Lines of Research

- Female references in teaching and literacy models throughout history.
- Women educators and/or researchers who have promoted advances in the care and study of teaching-learning styles.
- Women agents of change in the leadership of educational organisations.
- Teaching strategies to improve the visibility of women's contributions.
- Incorporating a gender perspective into the curriculum.
- Methodologies focused on female contributions in different fields of study.

Dr Khomotso Mashalane

Khomotso is a globally recognised humanitarian, philanthropist and women empowerment advocate. For over two decades, she has continued to be instrumental in empowering women from small capacities to leadership positions. Her key focus is researching issues concerning women in leadership, salary disparities between men and women as well as the numerous other social and business equity challenges women face.

Through her professional and academic endeavors, Khomotso has shown a great vision for humanity and humankind at a core level. Khomotso's leadership and training programs have empowered countless women to achieve success in their careers. She has helped women shatter the glass ceiling in various industries, from business to technology to health care. In addition to her leadership programs, she also provides scholarships and financial assistance to help women reach their full potential. Through her dedication and commitment, Khomotso has truly made a difference in the lives of many women around the world.

Khomotso Mashalane's vast and well-rounded career has spanned many different industries and disciplines. However, the one constant has been her dedication to serving and uplifting the women around her. Whether it's through her work as a business consultant, business coach, or even through her time spent teaching and mentoring young women, Khomotso has always put the needs of others first. This commitment to helping others has led her to become an expert in human resources, business planning,and personal development.

Breaking Down Barriers for Those With Invisible Disabilities

Linda Fisk

Today, one of the single best indicators of an exceptional work environment is a strong commitment to diversity and inclusion. When it's clear that an employer values every individual's contribution and all employees are provided with every chance to succeed, you'll find a more engaged, committed, loyal and high-performing workforce. When an employer focuses on individual abilities and rewards exceptional performance, the employees have the assurance of fairness and equity that diversity and inclusion initiatives were always meant to inspire.

Diversity definitions have now expanded to include less visible characteristics like parental status or religion. But today, leaders are not only focused on embracing the strengths of a diverse workforce, but they are incorporating inclusion strategies as well, clearly demonstrating their drive and commitment to engage the unique qualities and abilities that every single employee can bring to a job.

And while definitions of diversity in the workplace have now expanded to include religious beliefs, sexual orientation and even parental status – which are not visible differences – it's important to highlight that about one in ten people live with an invisible disability. And many times those invisible disabilities can impair their ability to work under normal conditions or participate in social activities at work. People with invisible disabilities can have dramatic limitations on typical work activities – and it can be difficult for coworkers to acknowledge, recognise and understand the disability.

Of course, it is the right of the individual to disclose their disability or not to their employer. Due to the social stigma directed at people with disabilities within the workplace and outside of the workplace, some employees with an invisible disability choose not to disclose their diagnosis. In fact, a recent study found that 88% of people with an invisible disability had negative views of disclosing their disability to employers from a fear of being labelled.

Invisible disabilities can range from epilepsy to dyslexia, hearing and vision impairment to chronic pain, PTSD to autoimmune compromised and diabetes, and mobility impairments to anxiety and depression. In the United States, 96% of people with chronic medical conditions show no outward signs of their illness. About a quarter of those with some sort of chronic medical condition have activity limitations ranging from mild to severe. In the time of COVID-19, the incidence of invisible disabilities are certain to grow as people confront the increasing number of physical and mental health issues.

It's important to note that if a person has a disability that does not mean they are disabled. Many living with invisible disabilities are still fully active in their work, families, sports or hobbies. Some with disabilities can work full- or part-time but may struggle to get through their day. Others may need assistance and have difficulty with daily activities which would make it difficult to maintain gainful or substantial employment due to their disability.

Everyone with a disability is unique, with varying challenges and needs as well as abilities, qualities and characteristics. But a lack of sensitivity to another's disability, especially an invisible disability, can create misunderstandings, resentments and frustration, worsening the situation. Coworkers may consider someone with an invisible disability to be lazy, weak, antisocial, incompetent, aloof or distant.

Those suffering from invisible disabilities should be offered the same considerations and protections as all other disabilities – no person should be discriminated against because of disability, whether it is hidden or visible. As leading employers recommit to nurturing a diverse and inclusive workplace, invisible disabilities should be identified, discussed and considered. When an employer focuses on individual abilities and provides a safe and inclusive environment for everyone, teams flourish, employee loyalty soars and performance skyrockets.

Inclusivity breeds employee support, builds morale and nurtures employee loyalty – even down through line operations where the message can still too often get lost. By focusing on individual abilities and rewarding exceptional performance, the company can engender the sense of fairness and just rewards that diversity and inclusion was always meant to instil.

Smart leaders will take hidden disabilities into consideration, reconfigure diversity and inclusion programs to meet the needs of all and become sensitive to the growing population suffering from invisible disabilities. Many of those who have seemingly recovered from COVID-19 are expected to face chronic health problems for the rest of their lives. Savvy leaders will rethink their diversity and inclusion programs to include invisible disabilities, giving those suffering appropriate accommodations and a safe place to disclose their unique disability.

Your diversity model can set you apart and offers a significant recruitment edge for your company. Your organisation can cultivate a reputation as offering a fair and equal playing field when it comes to career opportunity. That message provides a sustainable competitive advantage for your company and breeds industry excellence. It motivates every kind of talent in your business, supports external relationships with vendors and customers and it enhances your competitive position in the industry.

Your commitment to diversity and inclusion can provides a sustainable competitive advantage for your company – motivating every kind of talent in your business. Now more than ever, it defines the kind of corporate culture that we want to shape and cultivate in the next century.

Linda Fisk

Linda Fisk is a multi-award-winning leader, keynote speaker, bestselling author and university professor dedicated to amplifying and extending the success of other high-calibre business leaders. She is the founder and CEO of LeadHERship Global, a community of unstoppable women enhancing their leadership blueprint and embracing their power to be the best version of themselves – in work and life. In LeadHERship Global, Linda supports and guides ambitious, creative women to move in the direction of their purpose, their mission and their dreams with powerful connections, critical support, practical tools and valuable resources to show up, speak up and step up in their careers and personal lives.

Why Diversity is Important for Business

Raised in Chinoit

Naila Qazi

An Uphill Struggle

Being raised in Chiniot, a small, rural town in Pakistan, certainly wasn't easy. It was even more challenging if you were a girl being raised by a lower-middle-class, conservative family in a country where the social and cultural values clashed with opportunities for your gender. With little in terms of resources and a tough journey to keep myself in school, I had to fight tooth and nail to achieve everything I have.

According to the World Economic Forum (WEF)'s 2021 Global Gender Gap Report[1], the female labour force participation in Pakistan remains stuck at 22.6%, with women making up a mere 4.9% of senior business roles. Clear sex preferences, combined

1 weforum.org/reports/global-gender-gap-report-2021

with religious, cultural and social factors, make advancing in the business world as a woman nearly impossible. This, coupled with the lack of female role models, made things even more difficult for me. Without diversity and representation, it was hard to see myself in roles that simply didn't take women into consideration. This is especially prevalent when it comes to corporate environments. Yet, strength comes from challenges, and this drove me to strive for more.

Instead of accepting the position society had deemed fit for a woman, I did everything I could to keep myself in school. Whether it was doing chores, fetching water or running around looking after my younger siblings, I did whatever was necessary to continue my education and growth. Unfortunately, I had to make double the effort that men did to get the opportunities they got without even trying. Yet, this didn't stop me from reaching for the stars – it only made inequality and sexism clear to me in a way that pushed me to better myself and ensure I could change these circumstances for the next generation.

Success Amidst Adversity

While I struggled to find opportunities when I was younger, I worked hard to gain every advantage I could. When I grew up, things changed. I got married, migrated to Australia and started a family. However, I continued to work hard and completed a master's degree at the University of Melbourne at the same time to further my career and constantly learn. After completing my MBA in Sydney, and running a few businesses, I embraced travelling and eventually migrated to Canada.

Because of years in different countries like Pakistan, Australia and North America, my experience has given me a unique insight into the importance of a global mindset. As such, I value constant improvement and proving my worth by putting in the effort and contributing to all the companies I've been fortunate enough to work for. My foundations have been built on hard work and proving myself and have led to me becoming a global citizen who is passionate about education, inclusion and diversity.

Equity and Inclusion: Why They Matter

Diversity and inclusion aren't just about moral and social values. They're much more and are integral to any business, big or small. Exceptional talent comes from everywhere, and diversity brings about both economic and business advantages. Several bodies of research have made this exceptionally clear. Research from McKinsey[2] found that diverse companies tend to be more profitable. In fact, companies that embrace gender diversity were found to be more likely to achieve above-average profitability.

Furthermore, this doesn't stop at diversity itself – the level of diversity plays a huge role in a company's success. According to insights from McKinsey[2], not only were companies with more female executives more likely to outperform companies without female executives, but the percentage of executives made a significant difference. Those with more than 30% of female executives outperformed those with female executives that ranged from 10% to 30%.

It's also critical to note that the advantages of diversity don't stop at profitability – diversity also drives innovation. According to Harvard Business Review[3], research based on forty case studies, a survey of 1,800 professionals, and various interviews and focus groups revealed the importance of inherent and acquired diversity and highlighted a correlation between diversity and innovation.

2 mckinsey.com/~/media/mckinsey/featured%20insights/diversity%20and%20inclusion/diversity%20wins%20how%20inclusion%20matters/diversity-wins-how-inclusion-matters-vf.pdf
3 hbr.org/2013/12/how-diversity-can-drive-innovation

Companies with both types of diversity reported not only growth in market share but also capturing new markets.

Understanding the target audience flourishes in diverse teams and allows businesses to capitalise on market opportunities and expand. This is of the utmost importance when appealing to a global audience. Hewlett et al. (2013)'s research[4] showed that when a team consisted of at least one person with traits similar to the end user, the entire team understood the user better. When a team member shared a client's ethnicity, the team was 152% more likely to understand and serve the client's needs, highlighting the importance of inherent diversity.

Research has shown the importance of not only inherent diversity but also acquired diversity. According to Deloitte[5], diversity of thought can be a game changer for businesses. In addition to eliminating expert overconfidence and groupthink, diversity helps companies develop more creative processes and make better and more efficient decisions. Furthermore, employees can combine diversity of thought with technological innovations to solve challenging problems that may not have been previously considered. According to Harvard Business Review[6], more cognitively diverse teams solve problems faster, boosting both innovation and efficiency.

Diversity fosters innovation. Deloitte estimates that diversity in thinking and perspectives not only increases risk spotting and subsequent risk reduction by up to 30%, but also boosts innovation by approximately 20%[7].

Of course, while physical diversity is also an essential part of the conversation, diverse thinking can ensure better problem-solving,

4 hbr.org/2013/12/how-diversity-can-drive-innovation
5 www2.deloitte.com/us/en/insights/topics/talent/diversitys-new-frontier.html
6 hbr.org/2017/03/teams-solve-problems-faster-when-theyre-more-cognitively-diverse
7 www2.deloitte.com/content/dam/insights/us/articles/4209_Diversity-and-inclusion-revolution/DI_Diversity-and-inclusion-revolution.pdf

learning abilities and cooperation. It's not enough to simply hire minorities – to truly innovate, excel and expand businesses, it's essential to back diversity up with experiences that have shaped you and given you a unique perspective.

My Pakistani upbringing does just this. I'm not just physically diverse. Instead, coming from the background I've come from and achieving my goals despite the obstacles in my way has given me a perspective that no-one else has. When it comes to thinking outside the box and embracing ingenuity, it's the diversity of thought that gets you there.

Since a company is reliant on employees and talent to grow and prosper, hiring is an essential part of a company's success. With today's jobseekers thinking of diversity and inclusion as essential when applying for and accepting jobs, DE&I is no longer an option – it's critical if a company wants to attract and hire exceptional employees. According to Glassdoor's 2020 Diversity and Inclusion Workplace Survey[8], 76% of jobseekers state that diversity is an essential factor in them applying for positions and evaluating offers from companies. In fact, 37% of jobseekers go as far as to say they would not apply to companies that lack diversity in their workforce. Thus, if companies want to continue to hire experienced and desirable candidates, they must value diversity and take action to highlight this. If not, they risk alienating a sizable pool of talent.

Inclusion and What It Entails

While having a diverse workforce is essential, it's not the same as the organisational culture being inclusive. Many think of diversity and inclusivity as synonymous, but this could not be further from

---

8 glassdoor.com/blog/glassdoors-diversity-and-inclusion-workplace-survey

the truth. Someone once said that diversity is a given, but inclusion is a choice. I agree with this wholeheartedly.

While diversity is more about representation, inclusion is about the environment[9]. This involves all employees feeling a sense of belonging and being comfortable sharing their points of view and insights. In order to make an organisation inclusive, all must be afforded the same opportunities. From processes and behaviour to practices and symbols, every aspect of an organisation must back up claims of inclusiveness. This includes language, stories and rewards. Another valuable addition is the inclusion of leadership development programs that instil inclusive leadership skills in managers and supervisors.

Equity Within the Workplace

Equity means that everyone has equal access. Unlike diversity and inclusion, equity is about fairness and having the same opportunities despite the position one holds. All three are important to foster an open and accepting work culture and need to be taken care of simultaneously. Simply addressing one concern does not work. While they're all individually important, they're all necessary as a whole to truly improve workplace culture and ensure a company's success.

Bringing Change to the Corporate World or Organisational Culture

In order for a company to truly flourish, it must use DE&I strategies to create a diverse and inclusive organisational culture. I have worked at several global organisations for almost two decades and have seen many attempts to improve DE&I. The strategies

9   mckinsey.com/industries/public-and-social-sector/our-insights/
advancing-diversity-equity-and-inclusion

that I have seen work firsthand and make a marked difference in the company culture are the following.

Respectful Workplaces and a Culture of Acceptance

A major factor in improving workplace culture is fostering a respectful workplace and an environment where individuals and teams can thrive. However, many organisations have toxic cultures that can cost them valuable, diverse talent. According to Harvard Business Review, toxic cultures cost organisations in the US almost $50 billion every year[10].

Research examining toxicity in the workplace and the reasons behind diverse talent leaving their positions shows that many women of colour seek better opportunities because their talents and skills are not valued.

The first step in establishing a respectful organisational culture is carefully examining the current culture. An honest evaluation and taking employees' opinions into account is critical, as are creating effective options for providing feedback and submitting complaints.

Zero-Tolerance Policy Regarding Harassment, Abuse, etc.

Toxic workplace environments result in burnout and marginalisation. In many cases, toxic behaviour doesn't just go unpunished but is rewarded. According to HBR, women of colour aren't just 19% less likely to feel their work is valued – they're also 18% less likely than their white counterparts to feel supported by their managers[10]. Additionally, 60% of women of colour don't think the

---

10 hbr.org/2022/04/leaders-stop-rewarding-toxic-rock-stars

organisations they work at can adequately handle racist incidents. This results in losing diverse talent and high turnover rates.

Focusing on the short-term gain by rewarding those who engage in toxic behavior has a negative impact in the long run. Thus, companies must have a zero-tolerance policy when it comes to harassment, abuse, sexism, racism and other toxic values. While training and coaching are appropriate when individuals are not aware of the impact of their actions, repeat offenders must be dealt with, and incidents must be taken seriously. If not, an organisation will lose diverse talent and the advantages that this talent can bring.

Flexible Work Arrangements

Remote work became the new normal during the COVID-19 pandemic. Yet, although we have moved past lockdowns, remote work has not lost its appeal. An increasing number of organisations are embracing hybrid models of work. Research has shown that this isn't just a preference for employers – it's also something that's preferred by employees, especially people of colour. According to Harvard Business Review, 81% of Black knowledge workers in the US prefer a hybrid model of work[11].

One of the ways to support employees of colour is to make hybrid or remote work a choice and offer them flexibility. This is also helpful for those who cannot commute and single parents. That being said, it's not enough to simply offer remote work as an option – companies must actively ensure equality by not prioritising those who come into the office. It's critical to ensure that remote workers do not miss out on networking opportunities, performance evaluations, promotions and more.

Remote work is advantageous for both employers and

11 hbr.org/2022/02/why-flexible-work-is-essential-to-your-dei-strategy

employees. While it improves employees' work experience, it allows employers to choose from a more diverse group of candidates and gives them access to a wider pool of talent. According to the Future Forum, less time in the office has resulted in gains[11] such as Black employees having better relationships with coworkers (increase of 17%) and feeling a greater sense of belonging (increase of 24%).

Thus, offering flexible work options, eliminating proximity bias and creating equitable work environments can go a long way in furthering DE&I. If not, companies risk losing diverse talent. According to Harvard Business Review, 60% of Black employees are not satisfied with the flexibility they have[11] currently and may look for new jobs. In order to attract and retain talent, employers must embrace this new normal.

Leadership Alignment Across All Levels

DE&I initiatives don't just apply to low-level employees. They must have senior-level backing. This includes diverse hiring across many levels of an organisation. Instead of simply having female employees, it's important to have female presence at every level, including the executive level. It's only by aligning diversity amongst different levels that an organisation can start to embody the diversity and inclusivity it preaches. This is especially important since women and people of colour often put in more effort, and their work is not officially recognised or rewarded.

Accepting Responsibility for Hurt

No matter how careful and inclusive an organisation tries to be, there is a possibility of DE&I-related harm. However, while this may be inevitable, it's not something that should be ignored. Organisations must learn to accept responsibility for their role in the harm caused instead of expecting non-apologies to work.

According to Harvard Business Review, a sound apology isn't just one where the tone and delivery are paid attention to. Leaders and company executives must understand what they are apologising for and must take responsibility[12] for the harm they have caused.

This includes thanking those who bring issues to notice, creating a psychologically safe work environment, establishing a protocol where employees feel comfortable sharing feedback and sincerely apologising for the harm caused. Furthermore, whistleblowers must be protected from retaliation, and the incident must be addressed in detail. Instead of simply apologising for and acknowledging their mistakes, organisations must take steps to remedy the problem by dealing with it at the source.

Supporting Employee Wellbeing

While a number of companies may support their employees' wellbeing through health programs and have several DE&I initiatives, many do not realise that the two are interlinked. HBR claims that organisations must address 'the intersectionality of DEI and wellbeing'.[13]

According to the 2021 Employee Health Benefits Survey by the Kaiser Family Foundation, 83% of large companies offer health and wellness programs for employees[13]. Yet, it's not health alone that makes a difference and allows employees to perform their best. Companies must address wellbeing as a whole, including physical, emotional, mental, social and financial health.

One of the ways to support employees' wellbeing is by having inclusive narratives and openly discussing issues. According to HBR[13], Black Americans suffer 1.7 additional poor mental health days due to police killings. Minorities such as AIAN people are

---

12 hbr.org/2022/04/enough-with-the-corporate-non-apologies-for-dei-related-harm
13 hbr.org/2022/03/supporting-the-well-being-of-your-underrepresented-employees

more likely to suffer from chronic health conditions, and those in the LBGTQ community are more likely to suffer from mental health issues.

Programs that address health and wellbeing in the context of DE&I and addressing and discussing these topics openly can go a long way in ensuring the wellbeing and productivity of your employees. It's also imperative to provide managers with inclusive training so they have the necessary skills to help those under them. Since 45% of inclusion experiences depend on a manager's inclusive behaviours[14], this is an especially important facet to consider.

Other practices to keep in mind include using inclusive language throughout job descriptions and company memos, create and promote employee resource groups (ERGs), showcase employee stories and invest in programs and that think of wellbeing holistically.

Allyship

While 70-80% of employees either identify as allies or want to be allies[15], they do not always follow this up with action. Instead of simply empathising with those facing discrimination or negative experiences at work, the employee culture must consist of taking action and saying something to a higher-up. Whether it's racism, sexism or other negative actions, supporting colleagues and speaking up can make an immense difference in company culture.

---

14 hbr.org/2022/03/supporting-the-well-being-of-your-underrepresented-employees
15 mckinsey.com/industries/public-and-social-sector/our-insights/advancing-diversity-equity-and-inclusion

Psychological Safety

According to McKinsey[16], diversity has several advantages, including employees being 152% more likely to discover new ways of working and organisations being 47% more likely to retain employees. Yet, Harvard Business Review points out that companies cannot benefit from diversity without ensuring psychological safety[17]. Diverse teams may underperform because of communication challenges and members being unable to voice their opinions for fear of rejection or embarrassment.

For organisations to benefit from the various advantages diversity has to offer, they must embrace psychological safety and create an environment where everyone can be heard without fearing negative consequences. In fact, a study on sixty-two development teams across six companies showed that high psychological safety was positively associated with performance and satisfaction with team members.

To build psychologically safe environments that diverse teams can flourish in, organisations should focus on framing diversity positively. This includes framing meetings as opportunities to share diverse opinions and information instead of looking at them as opportunities for evaluation and judgement. It is also helpful to look at diversity and differences as valuable and advantageous, and bridging differences between team members by sharing information regarding goals, concerns and more.

Conclusion

There are more opportunities for women in the corporate world than before, and many barriers have been broken down. Yet, many still remain, especially when it comes to the perception of

16 mckinsey.com/business-functions/people-and-organizational-performance/how-we-help-clients/diversity-equity-and-inclusion
17 hbr.org/2022/03/research-to-excel-diverse-teams-need-psychological-safety

professional women. However, this isn't something we have to accept. It's something we have the ability to change.

According to McKinsey's 2021 Women in the Workplace report[18], corporate female representation improved throughout the previous year and despite the significant challenges brought forward by the COVID-19 pandemic. Yet, this representation was still lacking. In addition to women facing burnout, their work is often unrecognised, and there are large gaps in representation in different areas of the pipeline.

As a global leader in diversity and inclusion (D&I), I am an expert on the subject. My knowledge, compounded with my vast experience, has helped me see a better and brighter future for not only women, but all sorts of diverse groups. My roles throughout the years have included being a leadership expert, certified business coach and a change maker. However, the role I'm most proud of is that of being a mentor. By mentoring girls and other women, I'm able to provide others with a strong female role model and mentor that I never had when I was young or starting out. I am passionate about elevating women and other marginalised groups to leadership positions and instilling leadership attributes in them. By educating, supporting and mentoring women and other diverse groups, we have the ability to change the business world for the better.

Having worked to ensure this change in various companies, including Vale and Rogers Communications and the City of Toronto, I have valuable and proven experience in DE&I, strategising and implementing policies that help organisations grow and flourish. By improving diversity, equality and inclusiveness within a company, I can help maximise performance and ensure that an organisation can benefit from all the advantages that

18 mckinsey.com/featured-insights/diversity-and-inclusion/women-in-the-workplace

DE&I can provide.

This process may be complicated, but with the right help, it can be a major catalyst in transforming your organisation. My services include assessing the baseline, looking at the current gaps in DE&I within your organisation, and developing a comprehensive road map to fill these gaps and improve overall performance. In addition to establishing SMART goals, I aid in facilitating the implementation of these goals and adequate measurement and tracking techniques to keep abreast of progress and impact. With my help, you can adopt inclusivity and diversity, and benefit from the various advantages that come along with a diverse and inclusive environment!

Naila Qazi

Global mindset and technology-driven with extensive experience collaborating and leading multi-jurisdictional and cross-functional teams in North America, Australia, and The Middle East. A seasoned management coach and mentor who builds effective teams and change leaders.

   Recent Work:

- Workplace and Technology Transformation
- HR Transformation and Finance Transformation
- Organizational Needs Assessment, Qualitative & Quantitative Data Analysis and Reporting
- Enterprise Change Management & Corporate Communications
- Leadership Strategy Design, Curriculum Development, Implementation & Evaluation
- Coaching and Mentoring Capability Development

What sets me apart is my ability to collaborate, partner, consult, and maintain strong relationships with clients and stakeholders.

I grew up in a small village in Pakistan and eventually moved out to study in Melbourne. I did my MBA, got married, and had kids. Along with my studies, I also dabbled in different businesses, like restaurants, transportation, consulting, etc. My journey took me to various parts of the world; I have worked and lived on almost all continents. I had the opportunities to lead teams, projects, and large-scale transformations. There has been lots of learning along the way.

Chief Operating Officer
Shelli Brunswick

'Every great dream begins with a dreamer. You have within you the strength, the patience and the passion to reach for the stars to change the world.'

I wish I could claim credit for this quote as it resonates so deeply with me, but the quote comes from Harriet Tubman, a woman who escaped slavery to become a 'conductor' on the underground railroad, an abolitionist, a nurse, a spy, a scout, a voice for women and such an important role model to thousands, if not millions, of people. She did what no-one thought possible during the era in which she lived.

Flash forward to the period in which we are now living. More kids aspire to be YouTube stars than astronauts[1]. Let that sink in.

There is absolutely nothing wrong with being a YouTube star – especially if you are using that medium to make your mark

---

1 ourcommunitynow.com/lifestyle/kids-say-they-want-to-be-youtube-stars-more-than-astronauts-when-they-grow-up

on the world and share your voice. But given that space is the domain in which I work – one which is facing an enormous talent shortage – I hear a stat like 30% of kids want to be professional YouTubers vs. 11% who want to be astronauts, and my heart sinks a bit.

The space economy has exploded to $469 billion. In fact, it's set to reach $1 trillion before 2030, and it needs people to enable it to thrive and continue changing the world. But it's not just astronauts. The space economy requires participation from people of all walks of life, with myriad interests and experiences. The space economy needs you.

Why Space Matters

One of the reasons people – and women especially – perhaps don't think of space as a career is because they don't know how expansive, inclusive and impactful the space ecosystem can be. This is not their fault. Historically, the industry has not done a good job of promoting itself beyond space exploration.

In reality, space is about precision agriculture that helps feed a hungry planet and create food security for all. It's about environmental sustainability, solving our greatest challenges here on planet Earth, and it's about innovating ideas to better our daily lives. This requires the expertise of everyone from data scientists and engineers to welders, artists and English majors. Simply put, there is room for all!

Because the space ecosystem is so big, let me give you some concrete examples of advances that you might not think about in terms of space innovation. Remember the days when you couldn't leave home without your purse? Now, if you forget it, it's okay as long as we have our phones. They can do it all. Those little devices we can't live without came from the space industry: NASA imaging technology, GPS, battery strength, recharging capability, encryption and something we always want – connectivity. We want to be connected to the internet, to each other and to all our information on our apps. These are all space technologies.

What about during the pandemic when everyone went to work remotely? Zoom became a lifeline to the outside world and the critical space infrastructure is what makes companies like Zoom possible.

Let's look beyond tech. Space is also responsible for health care breakthroughs such as mammogram detection, eye surgery, pacemakers, laser angioplasty and so much more.

And after our experiences with COVID-19, everyone wants to breathe cleaner air, safe from contaminants – as well as germs from other people – when they go to the store, the airport or their offices. NASA-designed air filters are eliminating the COVID-19 virus and all the other 'stuff' floating around. Today, you will find such filters put to work in hospitals, laboratories, schools and even our own homes.

Want a healthy snack? Some entrepreneurs I got to know who were graduate students in Qatar, figured out how to make something delicious out of fruits and vegetables that would normally be thrown away, and they did it using space technology. As a bonus, they're helping the planet by reducing food waste and food insecurity with their snack revolution.

I could go on and on with examples of how space touches everyday life, but you get the idea. I could even go so far as to say the global space ecosystem matters more for Earth than what's 'out there'. That is not to say that outer space is not important but to emphasise that it also provides the most vital insights as to how we can live better, healthier lives on our own planet.

Space exploration and innovation must continue if we want

to keep advancing – and that's where you come in.

Defying the Odds

Throughout this book, there are tremendous examples of diverse groups of women changing the world. For the space economy to reach its potential, it needs diverse perspectives, and right now we, like other industries, are falling short.

Women, for example, made up half the US labour force, but they represented only 20% of employees in STEM-related fields prior to the COVID-19 pandemic[2]. And across the board, as people return to work, men have been able to recoup their jobs at a much faster rate than women despite women accounting for 63.3% of all job losses[3]. The numbers are disheartening for other minorities as well, but this translates to even fewer women in STEM-related fields than before despite an abundance of available jobs.

On top of this, companies hiring space technology workers still sometimes place an undue emphasis on traditional, fixed skills and degrees that align with outdated job descriptions. Instead of placing value on soft skills, proven problem-solving abilities and unconventional yet effective professional or educational backgrounds, companies miss out on potential candidates with much to offer.

Take military veterans as one example. A veteran who joined the military straight out of high school and led teams in combat or reconnaissance missions is highly proficient with GPS technologies and has practical experience with materials used to make uniforms for a variety of climates, but might not seem like a natural fit for a startup based on traditional requirements of the past, such as

2 ensus.gov/library/stories/2021/01/women-making-gains-in-stem-occupations-but-still-underrep-resented.html#:~:text=Women%20Are%20Nearly%20Half%20of,Only%2027%25%20of%20STEM%20Workers&text=Despite%20making%20up%20nearly%20half,and%20math%20(STEM)%20workforce.
3 nwlc.org/resource/men-recouped-losses-women-lag-behind/

college degrees in STEM or product design. Nevertheless, their skill competencies, perspectives and experiences could prove invaluable, and in fact, that veteran may be the best candidate for space technology jobs.

What I am pushing for is a change in how we think about workers, values and skill sets so that more doors open up to people who may not have thought of the space ecosystem as a place for them as well as non-traditional candidates who have something unique to offer. Space has room for all of us – I know because I'm an example of the new space workforce.

A Little Backstory

I joined the United States Air Force right out of high school. Even though the armed forces were dominated by men at that time, I saw it as a way to serve, see the world and earn a college degree that would not translate to a long-term financial burden. This was the right decision for me, as it influenced not only my thinking but also my drive and confidence in myself.

I decided to keep pressing forward, applying to become an officer despite having very few female role models who could show me what that might look like. And I faced another challenge: the Air Force wanted STEM professionals – I have a bachelor's degree in business administration. My odds of being selected as an officer were 12%.

Though I did not look like the typical applicant on paper, I refused to let that deter me. I applied more than once, and I was ultimately accepted as a space program manager after figuring out how to position my skills within the context of what the decision-makers were looking for. My tenacity and ability to encourage people to see beyond my résumé in order to understand my skills, hustle and willingness to put in the work launched what would become an incredible, delightfully unexpected career in space policy, leadership, collaboration and change-making.

Driving Change Forward

Along my winding career path, I've learned a lot that I hope to pass on not just to women and underrepresented groups, not just to policymakers and not just to the space industry. These buckets are so interwoven in my experiences and viewpoints that each now feeds the others.

On a macro level, I believe the biggest lessons I can share fall under being a 'global change-maker'. As I see it, global change-makers are leaders that are also servants and participants; they understand that by looking at the big picture, they can serve a greater good through their actions to elevate others. When applied at a global scale, this creates more inclusivity and lifts the entire ecosystem by bringing more voices, perspectives and solutions to the table.

All too often, leadership is focused on individual organisations and the employees within them. By contrast, the perspective of a global change-maker is expansive, collaborating across organisations locally, nationally and internationally. This exponentially grows ecosystems such as space, technology and entrepreneurship. It creates more access and opportunity to allow under-represented groups to participate in emerging industries and invites a diversity of ideas, people and regions of the world to join future growth sectors. At a time when divisiveness has become the norm, global change-makers strip away ego to unite and improve rather than isolate and tear down.

So, what does this look like in action? Space Foundation has created the Workforce Development Roadmap, which provides a framework for global change-makers to move to action within the context of growing the space economy.

The Workforce Development Roadmap is comprised of five pillars or entry points for individuals and organisations, meeting them where they are today and providing a path forward through programs and partnership. These pillars are:

Awareness

To increase innovation and offer greater opportunity, education and awareness of space technology, we need to go beyond traditional education – and the narrow scope of space exploration and tourism – to secure a viable future workforce for the space economy.

Right now, thousands of patents at NASA[4] alone are waiting for commercialisation, and enterprises across a broad spectrum of industries are actively seeking tech insertion of new commercialised products and services. But how do we empower companies to commercialise space innovations if they don't know that they exist – and if they don't have the workforce there to bring such innovations to market? Space Foundation is working hard to broaden such awareness through its programming and partnerships.

Access

There are a lot of misconceptions about the space industry, like it's an elite workforce reserved only for rocket scientists or that only a select few companies win contracts with space-related government agencies. These ideas need to change.

The space workforce spans STEM experts to labourers, and the future of the space economy is a collaboration of communities, public and private companies, government entities, colleges and

4 technology.nasa.gov/patents

individuals – opening pathways to all interested parties. Space Foundation endeavours to demystify access to space industries so that everyone can be a part of the space economy at any stage in their career. Its Space Commerce Institute team in particular engages with communities, entrepreneurs, small-medium businesses, educational institutions and incubators to determine needs and curate custom-tailored programs, workshops and events that further space technology innovation and open doors for participation and contributions.

To further break down issues of access, Space Foundation works closely to welcome underserved groups such as minorities, women and veteran-owned businesses to the community. The outlook for identifying additional demographics to serve includes people in traditional roles displaced by automation in changing work paradigms, aging workers or retirees.

Training

Careers are no longer linear, and technology is transforming workplace dynamics at a rapid clip. Compounding this uncertainty, traditional education cannot keep pace with the requirements of a fast-changing job markct. Recognising these changes, Space Foundation is a strong advocate for lifelong learning and making an investment in continued education throughout the career life cycle.

Space Foundation is piloting several custom-blended training programs that engage learners at any age or stage of their careers. Most are in collaboration with communities, corporations, governments and universities. Training environments range from DIY online training, live seminars and lectures to immersive and hands-on instruction and virtual learning programs, with an eye toward facilitating internships and apprenticeships in the future.

Connecting

Gaining entry to the space community, like many fields, is hastened by connections. As one of the most respected authorities on space since 1982, Space Foundation inherently has one of the deepest networks for connecting workforce candidates to space professionals and industry opportunities via its Space Symposium conference. Its massive reach spans the globe while also working at the local, regional and national levels to have a maximum impact.

We, and other organisations, need to leverage these connections to examine space issues from multiple perspectives, promote dialogue, conduct new business and focus attention on critical space issues. Partnerships are formed through connections, facilitating progress toward goals that benefit us all.

At the same time, individuals who want to work in or with the space industry must step up. As plentiful as opportunities are, people still have to put in a little effort. A job or sales deal is not likely to fall into your lap without attempting to network and prove your value.

Mentorship

This is the pillar closest to my own heart. I've said before that to achieve your career goals, every woman needs a mentor, a life coach and a champion. You may have more than one such person at each position, but it is the combination of these three key roles that is so powerful because each serves a different purpose. To build and retain a qualified workforce requires supplying mentors, life coaches and champions for today's youth, educators, young professionals, entrepreneurs and small businesses.

What do I mean by this? Mentors are focused on a very specific area in which you want to learn or improve. Think entrepreneurship, public speaking or budgeting. It's analogous to a position coach in sports. By contrast, a life coach focuses on the bigger picture, like how to make you a better leader overall. What are the human skills you need to develop? Then there are your champions. These are the leaders several levels above you, the ones who can inspire you and open the doors to help you reach the next level of an organisation.

You see, people are one of the most powerful levers we have – for better or worse. When each of these types of role models are in your corner, you can do anything! But when you don't have someone to look up to or bounce ideas off – or you are constantly being fed negative messages through industry representation – it can crush a career before it's even started. This is why we need leaders to act as servants, to pay their knowledge forward as an investment in the next generation. Space Foundation has created programs to cultivate mentors, life coaches and champions as well as to connect them with others who seek such models.

The Workforce Development Roadmap is not specific to our industry. We believe it will help us get where we need to go while providing incredible opportunities for women to do bold things. And this framework can be adapted and applied to other industries as well. I hope you will use it to become a mentor, life coach or champion on your own personal path to becoming a global change-maker.

In this regard, I would like to issue a challenge: dream big. Dream like Harriet Tubman did. Dream to change the world. And if you want to reach for the stars, not only is there room for you in the space ecosystem, but we need you.

Shelli Brunswick

Shelli Brunswick, chief operating officer of Space Foundation, brings a broad perspective and deep vision of the global space ecosystem – from a distinguished career as a space acquisition and program management leader and congressional liaison for the US Air Force to her current role overseeing Space Foundation's three primary divisions: Center for Innovation and Education, Symposium 365 and Global Alliance.

Advocating for space technology innovation and entrepreneurship, Shelli collaborates with government, commercial and educational sectors on initiatives for space commerce, young professionals, teacher development and space-inspired curriculum.

Brunswick's work to champion the inclusion of underserved groups stems from staying true to the values instilled while she was in the military: a passion to share her journey, give back to the space community and contribute to the development of the next-generation workforce. As a leading role model for women in space, Brunswick was selected as the 2021 Global Technology Leadership Award and 2020 Diversity and Inclusion Officer and Role Model of the Year Award by WomenTech Network, and a Woman of Influence by the *Colorado Springs Business Journal*.

Brunswick speaks at organisations and events around the globe to advance space technology innovation partnerships and collaboration, chairs Space Entrepreneurship and Leadership at Tod'Aers, chairs Space Tourism Society Africa and chairs G100 Space Technology and Aviation Wing. In addition, she is one of only fifty-four women worldwide to be selected by the United Nations as a mentor for its Space4Women program and is a World Business Angels Investment Forum senator for the USA and serves as the co-lead for their Global Women Leaders Committee board of directors. She is a founding advisory board member for WomenTech Network. She serves on the America's Future Series Space Advisory Board and sits on the board of directors for Colorado's Manufacturer's Edge.

The Future is Diverse

Karen McDermott

When I think of diversity I think of how the world is taking steps towards all inclusivity. Women are leading the way as women our feminine energy is no longer to be suppressed, but to be embraced. And yes, in my opinion, that has shifted the needle, a little, in a wonderful way. I'm sure there are still some people who don't agree, however, if we make the right decisions the way forward can be beautiful and balanced, where men and women, different cultures and all instances where there is segregation are finally equalized and instead it is embraced that we can play to our unique strengths.

I am one of those people who see everyone as equals. I always have. One of my earliest memories of how 'different' this all inclusive thinking was when I was about eight-years-old and a travelling family came to town and the children came to our school. I remember a girl starting our class, she spoke different and wore different clothes and had different mannerisms and there were people who picked on her. I stood up for her as I couldn't understand how someone couldn't empathise with her situation, I couldn't even imagine having to move around to different schools and live in a caravan, 2 weeks for school holidays at Bundoran beach every summer was enough for me. I was her friend for the few months she was at our school and I know that my kindness would have stayed with her a lifetime.

Humanity needs to step up to the mark and understand that it is in the best interest of our current and future generations to be the change.

I believe in a world that is all inclusive, where everyone is just thought of as 'people'. So, for me, diversity, especially from a female perspective, is showing up in our divine energy with the intent of making a difference in the world, while not worrying or being afraid of what other people think. We need to find the courage to show up and stand up, having a face-to-face conversation without worrying if we will disgruntle someone, even if we believe they may be at a higher level than us.

We must believe we can be equal in a face-to-face conversation because we are all on a journey in this life. We are born into the world with an equal shot. We may come from different backgrounds, but it doesn't mean we can't make a difference in our own lives and in the lives of others, no matter what denomination we come from. In fact, if we've come from less, we can be more of an inspiration because of how far we've come and the resilience we've built.

Resilience in spirit and resilience in mind, is a wonderful thing. We will all have traumas throughout our lives, and when we allow ourselves to process those traumas, we can awaken to new experiences. I believe we are reborn many times within our lifetime, that we don't just live one life. We rebirth and re-awaken, and in doing so, we live our lives to the fullest, showing others how to live theirs. When we focus on our path and our journey, it allows us to give the best of ourselves. So, shift into a higher gear and dominate.

The definition of diversity is to exercise power or influence over something or the state of being so controlled, as in, dominating a space. From a business perspective, and from my perspective and my way of doing business, it's about being very focused on the intentions I set, to be driven and purposeful in my actions and to build strong connections that support and sustain my goals and what I'm trying to achieve. Dominating in business, requires a strong network, and the strongest networks are those where people work together and lift each other up. They collaborate, not compete; celebrate and not put down. This is the type of diversity that the world needs.

Business; that's what I'm seeing thriving right now. I've seen a huge shift from a competitive model towards a powerful collaborative one. It's amazing when people work together. It can be magical when it happens. It's truly a testament to men and women who have shown up and shared that we can choose to come together and raise each other up. The comparison to that is pretty ugly if you ask me, which is when people pull each other down, but rising another person up is the most beautiful thing you will witness. It's knowing you've got each other's back and you're there to support each other, knowing we all have value to add. There's room enough in this expanding world for each of us, so let's celebrate each other to make a real difference to the lives of others.

I wanted to share a story from my own experience. I was called into a purpose, a purpose that was far bigger than me and anything I could have imagined for myself at the time. It was born from an epiphany and a calling to take action and write my story. The book I wrote became a catalyst into so much more. I really had to be courageous and honour the steps of what needed to happen, for my purpose to grow into reality.

After my journey of publishing my book, I knew I had to make a difference and so I decided to set a *really* big intention. I didn't worry about competitors, in fact, I didn't worry about anything else other than all my energy going into setting the intention and having the courage to follow each 'next' step. I had to have faith in the journey I was on and the steps I needed to make in order to move forward. So, I did that, one step at a time, and that's how I've ended up where I am today, ten years later, celebrating the wonderful journey and allowing the journey to be embraced while still working towards a destination.

Stories are important, they keep us connected!

While it's important to keep an eye on the destination, it's more important to be flexible because I have discovered that any destination is often surpassed tenfold to what you could have imagined when you set out. If you plan to be a leader in your industry it starts with inclusivity and then there is space for people to realise those goals and intentions are just part of the journey, there's so much growth that happens when you are moving towards what was once a dream and is now a reality.

There are a lot of struggles and breakthroughs that happen on the way, of course. And what I have seen from people who dominate a space, is that they don't see struggles and roadblocks as something to fear or run away from. They embrace struggles. They walk into the storm and hold steadfast in the knowing they have done the work needed to have the breakthrough. They stand strong in that space of knowing and have faith that their breakthrough is imminent, even when the struggle is uncomfortable.

I often talk about how important it is to not bail on the struggle, as so many people often do. When I see a fellow business owner turn away or give up whenever the struggle happens, it just breaks my heart. And the reason why, is because I *know* the breakthrough is imminent. They just have to withstand the storm before the calm. It's not a time for action. It's a time for being still and letting it pass through, allowing yourself to feel all the emotions.

If there's any advice I could give to business owners wanting to dominate in their space, it is exactly that. If the struggle is real and it feels like the ground is shaking beneath you, take the time to stop. Don't take action, just ride it out. Have the courage to stay the pace.

You know you've done the work, so have faith in everything you've done to that point and trust that you will be guided in any action you need to take. You will know when the clarity comes. Then once that unsettled struggle passes through, that is when you can do your happy dance and celebrate, because the breakthrough is there. And it's the biggest, most wonderful feeling when you've got a breakthrough to celebrate. Celebrate that moment, as it's a well-earned one – you've gone the distance and weathered the storm.

So, with my story, I weathered the storm. I did the uncomfortableness. I set my goal; my signpost goal of $1 million I thought was my destination, but it wasn't. I went on the journey to it and thoroughly enjoyed it, warts and all, but the journey is not over, it has led me to another signpost along the way.

There were many times when it was hard, but I never once thought I was going to bail. I had committed, I had made a sacred promise to myself to stick it out, to show up, not just for myself, but for others too. And when you do that, it's very powerful. People can see the purpose driven from your heart and the right people will always come along to help you on that journey.

And that's when amazing things happen.

Karen McDermott

Karen is an award-winning publisher, author, TEDx speaker and advanced law of attraction practitioner.

Author of numerous books across many genres – fiction, motivational, children's and journals – she chooses to lead the way in her authorship generously sharing her philosophies through her writing.

Karen is also a sought-after speaker who shares her knowledge and wisdom on building publishing empires, establishing yourself as a successful author-publisher and book writing.

Having built a highly successful publishing business from scratch, signing major authors, writing over thirty books herself and establishing her own credible brand in the market, Karen has developed strategies and techniques based on tapping into the power of knowing to create your dreams.

Karen is a gifted teacher who inspires others to make magic happen in their lives through her seven life principles that have been integral in her success.

Website: serenitypress.org & kmdbooks.com & mmhpress.com

Women Diversity & Media

Toni Lontis

According to Aneeta Rattan et el, in a 2019 article, 'Around the world, women are far less likely than men to be seen in the media. This gender-imbalanced picture of society can reinforce and perpetuate harmful gender stereotypes.'[1]

She further went on to state, 'As subjects of stories, women only appear in a quarter of television, radio and print news. In a 2015 report, women made up a mere 19% of experts featured in news stories and 37% of reporters telling stories globally.'

We would all agree that this needs to change!

Media, in all its forms, should serve the community. To do this effectively, the broadcasters, print and online media platforms must reflect the diverse range of perspectives and opinions of their audiences. It also means fostering the participation of ethnic and linguistic minorities, persons with disabilities and marginalised groups, to have their voices heard and actively contribute to media content creation and policy planning, according to UNESCO.

1 hbr.org/2019/06/tackling-the-underrepresentation-of-women-in-media

In this day and age, the shaping of our beliefs, values and perceptions are driven by news media, social media and the vast audiovisual sectors. These sectors are a window to new ways of thinking, changing attitudes and challenging stereotypes. The #metoo movement contributed to the current changes we are seeing across many sectors, including media, in the treatment and portrayal of women in media, but there remains a way to go. The gender gap in representation of women remains today and is especially relevant in women's lack of representation in leadership and management positions, access to employment, funding and equal pay. There is a further worsening of the situation when we look to those women belonging to less privileged portions of society and the discrimination they experience increases their suffering and under-representation.

The responsibility of media to question the stereotypical views of women and girls and encourage diversity across all media platforms is inherent. Many of the world's global organisations are embracing the opportunities to encourage diversity. They are leading by example with policy, frameworks, programs and education to include woman and the diversity in what they bring to the world.

In the media, men are often portrayed as adventurous, dominant and sexually aggressive, while women tend to be portrayed as young, beautiful, emotionally passive, dependent and sometimes unintelligent. In Western media, women are expected to value youth, sexuality and beauty, while men are taught to value dominance and power. These stereotypes portrayed by media are not the norm and are harmful, not just for women but the diverse population of humanity.

There has been limited change in the last ten years, but whilst progress is slow, women can and need to be encouraged to do more, to use their voices, their presence and their wisdom to drive change – particularly in media.

The lack of representation of women in traditional news media is reflected in digital news. Only 26% of online news reports are for women. Only 4% of traditional news stories explicitly challenge gender stereotypes. The serious shortage of female media staff is one of the factors that has played an important role in this very statistic.

Women's full and equal participation in all aspects of society is a basic human right. In all parts of the world, the representation of women is low. Norms and traditions are related to patriarchy or in many instances, sequences are far-reaching with detrimental, negative consequences on the personal, economic and future wellbeing of women and girls, their families and the community at large.

Building a sustainable future for all means leaving no-one behind. Women and girls are critical to finding solutions to the biggest challenges we face today and must be heard, valued and celebrated throughout society to reflect their perspectives and choices for their future and that of the advancement of humanity.

How many more generations are needed for women and girls to realise their rights?

When it comes to equality of men and women in news media, progress has virtually ground to a halt. According to the largest study on the portrayal, participation and representation of women in the news media spanning twenty years and 114 countries, only 24% of the persons heard, read about or seen in newspapers, television and radio news are women. A glass ceiling also exists for women news reporters in newspaper bylines and newscast reports, with 37% of stories reported by women as of 2015, showing no change over the course of a decade.

Despite the democratising promise of digital media, women's poor representation in traditional news media is also reflected in digital news, with women making up only 26% of the people in internet news stories and media news tweets. Only 4% of traditional news and digital news stories clearly challenge gender stereotypes. Among other factors, stereotypes and the significant underrepresentation of women in the media play a significant role in shaping harmful attitudes of disrespect and violence towards women.[2]

Like other forms of media, film and television have a powerful influence in shaping cultural perceptions and attitudes towards gender and are key to shifting the narrative for the gender equality agenda. Yet, an analysis of popular films across eleven countries found that 31% of all speaking characters were women and that only 23% featured a female protagonist – a number that closely mirrored the percentage of women filmmakers (21%).

The gross under-representation of women in the film industry is also glaringly evident in critically acclaimed film awards. In the ninety-two-year history of the Oscars, only five women have ever been nominated for the Best Director Award category, and one woman – Kathryn Bigelow – has ever won. Jane Campion remains the only woman director to have won the Cannes Film Festival's top, most prestigious prize, the Palme d'Or, in its seventy-two-year history. The only other women to have received the prize – but jointly – were actresses Adèle Exarchopoulos and Léa Seydoux with the movie's male director Abdellatif Kechiche. If a picture is worth a thousand words, the message is worth a million: if we are to shift stereotypical notions of gender and reflect women's realities, we need more women in film, on-screen and off-screen.

2 The Global Media Monitoring Project (Data as of 2015); Report of the UN Secretary-General E/CN.6/2020/3

The emergence and fast proliferation of COVID-19 created the implementation of the sixth world media watch project (GMMP) the foremost and most encompassing since the initiative's origin in 1995. Yet, despite the pandemic, the media sample was the best ever. The analysis by 116 groups with 172 stories printed in newspapers, broadcast on radio and TV, and disseminated on news websites and via journalism tweets.

25% of stories within the sample carried a coronavirus sub- or principal theme. A tweak within the methodology created potential to research the stories on the classic GMMP major topic classes of politics and government, economy, science and health, social and legal, crime and violence and celebrity/media/arts and sports. The GMMP 2020 topics' structure added a seventh major topic 'gender and related', which clustered stories specific to harassment, rape, #metoo and similar gender-specific news.

All things remaining equal, it'll take a minimum of an additional sixty-seven years to shut the typical gender equality gap in journalism and news media. That's astounding and simply not okay.

In 2015, the gap remaining to full gender equality is reported as seventy-two years, so the 2020 result signals consistency within the slow accumulative pace of modification over time. Full gender equality on numerical counts, however, is not improvement within the quality of journalism from a gender perspective.

At the worldwide average level, it is thought that media is presently at the midway point to gender parity in terms of subjects and sources.

Between 2015 and 2020, the needle edged forward to twenty-five within the proportion of subjects and sources United Nations agency and is most visible in broadcast journalism.

Despite their three-point decline within the proportion of

female subjects and sources since 2015, journalism stayed the most effective performer worldwide. European journalism has created the foremost vital progress on this indicator since 1995 and the Pacific region media within the past five years. Unfortunately, Africa's media has stagnated because the remainder of the regions have improved by three to twelve points across the quarter century.

Implications of #metoo

The pattern of under-representation of women and girls, even in stories that concern them, is still not spilling over in news content on gender-based violence.

Stories on gender-based violence (GBV) hardly make the news of the day, and once they do, women are severely under-represented as subjects and sources. A sample of the stories within the total sample were coded below the 'gender and related' major topic that features news on numerous sorts of gender violence against women.

Furthermore, that women and girls are under-represented in stories regarding molestation, rape and regulatory offence. Notably, throughout COVID-19 times, these acts have reached epidemic proportions. This signals a significant deficit in journalism answerableness to female-specific crime reported in media. This severe under-representation in stories takes place in newspapers within which women are simply not represented adequately.

There are multiple and additional dangers in visibility and voice for minority and traditionally marginalised women and girls.

Teams in eighty-one of the collaborating countries took the chance to gather information on indicators of interest within the national context. The variety of those indicators created the ability to take the results from a victimisation and intersectional lenses, to grasp journalism treatment of subjects and sources on the idea of their alternative identities like race, religion, class/caste, immigration and incapacity standing.

The failure to increase the chance for a lot of women to inform their own stories in their own words, to inform the stories that are vital to them and also to a broad variety of individuals, compromises the worth of the news to its multiple and various publics. The failure to represent the variety of individuals and opinion in society, not solely has implications for public discourse and decision-making, it additionally plays a role in geologic processes of trust in news journalism.

Appreciable Gains in Women's Presence as Authoritative Sources

Women's voices as spokespersons have risen by eight points since 2005, and as specialists by seven points within the same amount of time. In recent years, varied initiatives to have knowledgeable female opinion and perspective have increased round the globe and media organisations are visibly creating efforts to diversify their experts' pools, responding to external pressure. It is also revealed that diversity is taking a higher priority in internal business efforts to try and provide higher numbers of female experts. The last five years have seen the highest rise in numbers of female experts in media.

In keeping with the historical patterns, women are still under-represented as expertise suppliers (42% in media, 41% public opinion givers).

Gender-Lens-Deficient Pandemic News

Coverage

Gender equality within the world is progressing, however, within the news and news media it still lags behind gender equality within the physical world.

While understanding and the acknowledgement of women's contributions have grown within the lived world, this still doesn't translate to the world of journalism. During the pandemic, only 27% of health specialists showing up in coronavirus stories were women. With women accounting for 46% of the labour force in health care, this is less than the world average given in labour force statistics. Of the persons delineated as homemakers, women make up virtually seven in ten, just like the 2015 findings. Similarly, their ranks among the jobless as delineated in news reports have risen by eight points within the past five to twenty years. In reality, the international bank for reconstruction and development modelling of the ILO's sex-disaggregated labour force statistics suggests that state rates have reduced for men by 0.4 points and for women by 0.5 points since the year 2000.

Gendered Favouritism Within the News

2020 was additionally the primary year of the world COVID-19 pandemic, wherever maturity was thought of a standard divisor for being in danger. However, folks within the oldest age bracket seldom got attention within the news – in particular women over the age of eighty years old became invisible in news reporting.

Overall, in print news, men fifty years and older are well represented, 42% of women within the news belong to the present age bracket. The best represented age class for women is in the thirty-five to forty-nine years age bracket, whereas men peak in visibility at fifty to sixty-four years of age. In newspapers and on TV, women over the age of fifty became a lot more invisible.

Following stagnation between 2005 and 2015, women's visibility as reporters has raised by three proportion points overall across print and broadcast news.

Currently, four out of ten stories in journalism are reported by women. Within the past twenty years, women's newspaper byline credits have been raised by eleven points, their visibility in newscasts has raised eleven points as well.

A comparison between print and digital newspapers reveals that stories by female reporters are distributed a lot less equally across the foremost topics online and offline, compared to those by men. The newsman gender gap is precisely constant in Asia, Europe and the Pacific region. The news and media industry have progressed slower than the remainder of the globe.

The Sex of the Newsman Matters for the Gender Dimensions of the Dtory

GMMP findings across time indicate that female reporters are a lot more likely than men to report on women subjects and sources. In 2015, the results advised that the gender supply choice gap was narrowing, however, within the 2020 wave, the gap has doubled.

So, What Does This All Mean?

With research suggesting that many women remain locked out of top roles in media and entertainment, we need a more diverse cast of women in the higher leadership levels of media and entertainment to change this. With women among the largest consumers of film and television, they represent a key demographic for this industry and the advertisers and sponsors that support it – this alone should be a key driver of change.

The research also suggested that the women in the industry believed that they were subjected to very different standards to men. Women experienced more microaggressions than women in other industries. All of these points could be addressed by some of the initiatives following:

- Appoint more women to board positions within the industry. Everyday Women's Network has an all-female advisory board with members from diverse backgrounds and industries providing expert advice.
- Establish senior-sponsorship programs. Sponsorship is crucial to career advancement for both men and women, but research shows they often have networks of different sizes.
- Create and commit to a culture of accountability. Ensuring that people at the top of the organisation are accountable for diversity and inclusion can help shed light on the lack of women in leadership positions within the media and entertainment industries.
- Ensure fair work practices within media companies. By creating and establishing HR processes and practices, combined with appropriate and fair evaluation criteria for senior leaders, managers and staff will assist with the breakdown of entrenched systems that have led to unequal representation at senior levels.
- Establish a systematic training program to combat biases. Cognitive biases can creep into performance evaluation and hiring processes at all levels. To help mitigate these biases, companies should offer unconscious-bias training at important decision-making junctures – for instance, in the case of hiring or promotion decisions.
- Listen to a woman's perspective. The media and entertainment industry are prime industries to ask and record the voices of women. A good way to understand how to create more

inclusivity in this sector is to learn from the women who have risen to leadership roles despite the obstacles in their way.

- Enlist men as allies. The research revealed a significant awareness gap between men and women in media and entertainment with regard to noticing biased behaviours in the workplace.

Given the nature of the media and the entertainment industry's ability to influence culture at large through its production of film, video and news publications, it is important for this industry to pay close attention to inclusion principles. As this report suggests, progress has been made, but there is more work to be done. I will lead the way by heralding the arrival of female-led global TV network, Everyday Women's Network, focused on supporting the diversity of women's voices and their creative perspectives and be the change we need to see. I encourage you all to do the same.

Toni Lontis

International radio and TV host, bestselling co-author, author, speaker and visionary, Toni Lontis quietly entered the entrepreneurial world in 2019, post publication of her memoir, *Resilience*.

After thirty-five years in nursing, from clinical practice to running her own nurse consultancy company, Toni wanted to write a book about what it takes to heal from dysfunction and trauma in her own life to create heart-centred impact and help heal others.

With the publication of the book came the audiobook production, and Toni was introduced to the power of the spoken word. A chance conversation led to a meeting with an American media company CEO and Radio Toni was born.

From these humble beginnings grew a love of interviewing businesses and people about life, business and the universe. Her intuitive interview style has taken the world by storm.

Toni now has multiple live streaming TV shows and a series of co-hosted business shows. She has just launched her own TV network, Everyday Women's Network, and is hoping to launch its partner network, The Everyday Network, in 2023, proving age, dysfunction and disability should never be a barrier to following your dreams.

Finding a Seat at the Leadership Table

Lisa Levy

Being the 'Only' Sucks

Over the last few decades, women have progressed in leadership roles within the corporate world. However, the workplace still isn't equal; this progress often occurs in the entry to middle management levels. Thus, we are still faced with the real possibility of being the 'only' in our team.

The pressure of being an 'only woman' is palpable. Although it comes with the benefits of being noticed and remembered at all times, it isn't easy. You'll constantly fight harder to have your voice heard and ideas honoured. You tend to have a fair share of subtle, if not loud, forms of biases making it hard to navigate male-dominated team dynamics. Compared to our male counterparts, our competence is questioned and our authority undermined. For us, there will always be a particularly difficult person in the room who seems resistant to our ideas, or they need to hear what we have to say multiple times and from other people. I certainly did when I became an information technology director. I was the only woman sitting at the table, which didn't bother me – until I experienced the effect of being 'the only'. It happened at our first team meeting; I inadvertently challenged my direct supervisor's approach and the logic he used for a particular opportunity.

After the meeting, he pulled me aside and instructed me that under no circumstances should I say anything in front of the group that could be seen as a criticism or a lack of support for him. My brain exploded! I left the conversation feeling deflated, but I took immediate action and built allies among my peers outside our formal meetings. I planted seeds of ideas with my direct supervisor – allowing time for him to process the ideas and then promote them to the group as if they were his. During my five years in the role, I helped him grow into the CIO of the organisation – the whole time taking criticism and blame for anything that did not bring him glory.

Alongside this comes the feeling that you must continually prove yourself and your gender in general. Being the 'only woman' in a male-dominated industry comes with an unspoken expectation that you represent *all women*. Everything we do stands out and is perceived to represent our identity, i.e. *all women's* abilities, qualities, needs and personalities. Therefore, when we fail, there is a worry that people will think all women will fail in that role, that the 'woman experiment' didn't work.

Not to mention the few or no mentors (of similar gender) above you who have broken the ceiling before you and can help you. As such, it can be more than just lonely and hard to be 'one of the few' or 'only' women in leadership roles.

Unfortunately, these and many more are the continuous reality of many women in the corporate world. Such biases and microaggressions leave these women feeling like outsiders when all they want to do is fit in. Figuring out how to change these ingrained behaviours is the greatest challenge women experience. It requires finding the strength to directly address potentially harmful behaviours to create a better team environment for everyone.

Challenges Entering Into Management Roles

Women across all industries and organisations worldwide have come a long way regarding workplace equality. We continue to face diverse forms of biases that pose a never-ending barrier to our advancement in the workplace, from discrimination in every unit to lack of support, 'ignored' harassment, under-representation in C-suite roles, subtle biases, etc. Unlike our male counterparts, we are always faced with the hard choice of first breaking the glass ceiling to succeed. This battle has been going on for decades, and the big question is: when will we ever get there?

Take for instance, women of colour: we see today's experiences of these women facing several kinds and frequencies of microaggressions as they did two years ago. Compared to their white counterparts, they tend to remain on the receiving end of disrespectful and 'othering' behaviour from their supervisors and colleagues. Irrespective of the trends and talks about women's equality in the workplace, there are still many lingering effects of the past; women are promoted to managers at far lower rates than men, and women of colour still lose ground in representation at every level, especially in-between the entry-level and the C-suite.

An analysis of the representation of women in corporate America, done by McKinsey in partnership with LeanIn.Org, showed that for every one hundred men promoted to manager, only eighty-six women are promoted, which implies that there are far fewer women promoted to higher levels. This analysis also showed that although the 'few' women in leadership roles are rising as stronger leaders and are doing more to support their teams as compared with men at the same level, their work, especially in building inclusive workplaces, isn't truly prioritised by most companies, hence they tend to go unrecognised and unrewarded.

This inadvertently has concerning implications, not just for women but for the organisation in general. Companies risk losing the leaders they need right now to trigger a reckoning on diversity, equity and inclusion. The events of the recent decade have heightened the focus on workplace inclusion, thereby putting extraordinary pressure on companies and employees to reflect these changes since DEI is a key area of focus in promoting employee wellbeing. When managers support employee wellbeing and companies prioritise DEI, employees are happier, less burned-out and less likely to consider leaving their jobs.

With the foundation for sustained progress at more senior levels, these women leaders can bring about more results in both their work productivity and performance and bring about the needed change. They are DEI champions – compared to their male counterparts, women at the top position are more involved with the concept of inclusion. Studies have shown that they not only do more in taking more consistent action to promote employee wellbeing, but they also take on the extra work that comes with advancing the concept of inclusion. They have been known to help team members navigate work-life challenges while checking in on their overall wellbeing and ensuring that their workloads are manageable.

These women also dedicate more of their time than men to DEI work that falls outside their formal job responsibilities. For instance, they organise DEI events, support employee resource groups and recruit employees from under-represented groups. More so, they are twice as likely to show up as more active allies to women of colour, educate themselves about the challenges these women face at work and speak out against such discrimination.

Despite all this, relatively few companies formally recognise employees who go above and beyond in these areas – and this needs to change. Overlooking critical work around employee wellbeing and DEI has serious implications: it hurts women who invest disproportionate time and energy in these priorities. And it hurts companies and all employees because progress is rarely made on undervalued efforts.

However, when managers see the value of women leaders' contributions, believe DEI is a high priority for their company and support employees who have strong allies, there will be a lot of work for women leaders who do more at driving better outcomes for all employees.

Burnout Is Real – and It's Worse for Women

Before the outbreak of COVID-19, the average working American woman was highly stressed. This is because, alongside fighting for our equality, we are left with a system that hardly recognises or appreciates our efforts. So, we must do twice as much as our male counterparts to be heard or seen.

With the emergence of the pandemic, such stress has doubled in the last two years due to the mental strain coupled with the social context of corporate American work systems. This is the new reality for working women across various organisations as they personally and painfully have to struggle with burnout.

Several points of data show that over 42% of women report being burned-out, implying that we are all just 'hanging in there'. The level of burnout has reached alarmingly high levels as these women are now significantly more burned-out—and increasingly more so than men – than they were before. As a result, many women have made career and life decisions driven by their experiences with burnout over the past year. Some have taken time off work because of mental health challenges or have started seeking new, more flexible working patterns; for others, it implies downshifting their career by switching jobs or leaving their employers or the workforce entirely.

Women are fighting so hard, but it feels like the odds are against them. One part of our story is the effect of our representation in corporate America, for which its crisis is far from over. And another has to do with our mental and physical health. The feeling of burnout is more like a battle most women have waged internally throughout the pandemic and even afterwards. They deliver the performance and business results needed but at a great personal toll.

Across talk of these, companies who are nonchalant about this are heading for loss as they face a potential talent crisis if these women make a move out of an organisation. With such a move, these organisations will likely lose half of their women senior leaders – the major drivers of DEI – which would take them back decades. Despite this added stress and exhaustion, they continue to make important gains in representation, especially in senior leadership.

Top leaders and managers of every organisation have an important role in fighting burnout. This is because each of their actions significantly impacts employee burnout and wellbeing.

Therefore, they need to focus on three key areas:

- Modelling work-life boundaries.
- Supporting employee wellbeing.
- Ensuring that performance is evaluated based on results.

Although several organisations have begun addressing burnout by introducing health benefits and offering more paid leave, among other efforts, burnout is still on the rise, especially among women. Undoubtedly these steps have led to better outcomes for all employees, and they have likely played a key role in allowing many women to remain in the workforce, but they are not enough!

More bold steps need to be taken to address burnout across corporate America. The American corporate world should know that there is no easy fix, so the continued investment is critical. Companies must continually demonstrate a strong commitment to the wellbeing of these women. Alongside these, they also need to make strides in recognising and rewarding the women leaders who are driving the progress of DEI by:

- Highlighting that engaging in deep cultural work is required to create a workplace where all women feel valued.
- Exploring creative solutions and opportunities to expand on the successful policies and programs they have already established and trying new approaches.
- Establishing new norms and systems to improve women's work experiences daily. You have to put it in the structure that'll pass the right message of inclusion across, else they will continue to struggle if the cadence and expectations of their work feel flawed.
- Embracing flexibility in work hours so these women can take more time off and step away from work. They shouldn't feel the need to be available for work twenty-four seven or work long hours to get ahead.
- Explicitly defining expectations and boundaries for these women if they work remotely or work flexible hours.

It's also important that managers actively monitor employees for signs of burnout and adjust workloads as needed. Although some managers are stepping up on this front – especially women – most employees report that their manager doesn't check in on their wellbeing or help them shift priorities and deadlines regularly. This suggests that rather than generally asking them how they're doing, managers need to consistently check in with their team individually to rate their stress and exhaustion on a one-to-ten scale.

Finally, there is a need for these organisations to impress upon managers. Hence, they become aware that the work they do to support employee wellbeing is critical to the health and success of the business. Efforts toward reducing burnout for these women must be tied to concrete outcomes, including performance ratings and compensation.

'Double Onlys' Experience Is Exponentially Worse

After several years of increased focus on DEI and racial equity in corporate America, women are still under-represented in top positions in most organisations. More like a 'sheep amid wolves', these women working in male-dominated industries are left vulnerable to flawed perceptions and biases of their male bosses and colleagues daily. The most significant of these biases involves multiple and intersecting identities that profoundly compound other challenges women face at work.

Being the only woman and the only person of their race or ethnicity in such a workplace exposes these women to certain forms of bullying and microaggressions at similar relative frequencies, which leaves them feeling downcast and unproductive at the end of the day.

A study undertaken by LeanIn.Org and McKinsey & Company showed that 64% of women experience microaggressions daily, making it a workplace reality. They are more likely than other women to have their judgement questioned in their area of expertise and be asked to provide additional evidence of their competence. One-third of lesbians feel they can't talk about themselves or their life outside work. They are more likely than other women to hear demeaning remarks about themselves or others like them in the workplace. Thus, they feel discouraged from talking about their personal lives at work.

These negative experiences of these microaggressions often add up. As their name suggests, they seem small when dealt with one after the other. But when repeated over time, they tend to have a major impact, taking a heavy toll on these women. For instance, women who regularly experience microaggressions get burned-out as they are less optimistic and have issues trying to concentrate at work as a result of stress.

An effective measure to reduce these challenges for women of minority groups is to aid an allyship from their white colleagues, i.e. white employees consider themselves allies to women of colour at work. This includes speaking out against bias or advocating for new opportunities for women of colour. When women of colour become aware of having strong allies, they become happier at work, feel less likely to be burned-out and are less likely to consider leaving their companies. However, not more than three-quarters of white employees consider themselves allies to women of colour at work, and fewer consistently take key allyship actions.

This shows that although white employees recognise that speaking out against discrimination is critical, they are less likely to recognise the importance of more proactive, sustained steps such as advocating for new opportunities for women of colour and stepping up as mentors and sponsors.

Given the day-to-day challenges, it's not surprising that women of colour face greater challenges and are more committed to seeing that their company substantially follows through on DEI goals.

Gender Parity In Eighty Years Is Absurd. Diversity of All Types Is Necessary Now!

The challenges of DEI can't be fixed in a day. However, without an intentional action towards alleviating these challenges we will remain where we are without any feasible progress. Below are the major steps that an organisation can and should take in regards to creating a DEI environment.

Practices

Currently, several companies are taking more steps to reduce bias in hiring. However, they should apply that same rigor to the performance review process. This is a great way to ensure equitable promotions for women, especially women of colour. Since women's experiences of biases and microaggressions are shaped primarily by their interactions with managers and colleagues, these practices should birth a culture that fully embraces and leverages diversity so that all employees become empowered to be part of the solution.

Alongside these, senior leaders need to fully and publicly support DEI efforts by modelling inclusive leadership and actively participating in training and events related to DEI. In doing this they send a powerful signal about the importance of this work.

Representation

Alongside putting in place the practices that ensure DEI culture, these organisations need to also track the representation of these women through hiring and promotion outcomes. This implies that women, especially women of colour, shouldn't be overlooked during hiring and promotions. If there are gaps in the rate at which these women are hired and promoted compared to other employees, then adjustments need to be made.

Accountability

Regarding accountability, efforts to accelerate progress for all women need to be doubled. Although most organisations say that they treat DEI with great priority, only a two-thirds of these organisations hold their managers and senior leaders accountable for progress on DEI goals.

Moreover, in the companies that say they hold leaders accountable, less than half factor progress on diversity metrics into performance reviews and far fewer provide financial incentives for meeting these DEI goals. Hence, they are much less likely to produce results.

Therefore, there is a need to ensure DEI initiatives are appropriately resourced across the organisations where all stakeholders get to participate in ensuring such goals. At the same time, they are also being held accountable for progress on DEI efforts.

Efforts to promote gender equality have come a long way in gaining attention and catalysing change, but there is still a long way to go. Although women are now a part of the workforce there is still a significant lag in fulfilling the promises of equality at work, with a hundred-year gap from female representation in leadership to pay equity. Online campaigns centred specifically on women continue to spring up and are now perceived as noise that masks the lack of real action and progress. Attaining gender parity in the future is ambiguous and absurd. Diversity of all types is necessary now – the onus is on us all to take bold steps and real actions that can guarantee the needed results.

It shouldn't stop with the hashtags on social media, but the DEI should physically penetrate every unit of a corporate organisation. There should be a wave of investment in all aspects of diversity, equity and inclusion across the corporate world. Companies need to ensure that women of diverse identities are well represented. This can be majorly attained by creating a culture that fully leverages the benefits of diversity – in which women and all employees feel comfortable bringing their unique ideas, perspectives and experiences to the table. When the minority within an organisation are respected and their contributions are valued, they are more likely to be happy and loyal to their jobs and to feel connected to their coworkers.

Lisa Levy

Lisa L. Levy is the Founder and CEO of Lcubed Consulting, a firm that helps organizations elevate through strategic goal achievement.

She and her team teach the Adaptive Transformation™ framework to savvy business leaders who want to build agility into their operating model to continuously Adapt and Thrive!

She is the #1 bestselling author of *Future Proofing Cubed* and contributing author to *The Gift of the Universe through Women that Lead*. Lisa is frequent guest expert on multiple media outlets, and speaker at business executive conferences.

Diversity in Business

Sarah Blake

Whether you are a business leader, entrepreneur or community advocate, the chances are that you have had to face barriers to your professional or economic growth. If you are from a gender or culturally diverse background it is even more likely that you have experienced some form of discrimination or disadvantage along the way. For many of us, it feels like we have talking about the benefits of diversity in business, community, and life, and yet here we are still having this critical conversation.

So why does diversity matter to me personally? My family on both my mother and fathers' side fundamentally valued community in all its messy forms. Both hard working farming families, they cared about how people and country were valued and were never really interested in the status of the person. In some ways they were ahead of their time. Doing environmental interventions before it was a thing, providing access to the first nations people whose land had been taken off them. Neither family had much but always gave to their communities in the best ways they could. It taught me that it doesn't matter what you look like or how much money you have – what matters is treating others with respect. They also taught me, in different ways that actions matter. Sometimes we must use our voice and sometimes we must put our actions into practice. It is these foundational lessons that have shaped my own perceptions about people and drawn me to learn, discover and experience difference without fear.

I think perhaps this curiosity is what has driven me to grow and create the company I now have. It has certainly inspired my vocational ambition to help people at a global scale navigate hard conversations without fighting. It is this deep sense of 'connection' that helps me hold people in conflict with a presence that brings a calm, steady influence.

As a conflict strategist, my job is to elevate leadership decision-making when there is confusion, conflict, or change. For me diversity isn't a nice to have, it is a normal and necessary part of life and I want to unpack the language of this with you. But I also know that for many people diversity – of thought, of background and interests often causes problems.

So, I want to start this conversation about diversity with a focus on the power of language.

In the business world, we are used to recognising the value of diversification. The adage "don't put your eggs in the one basket" rings true on an instinctual level. The business world understands that sustainability requires us to spread our investments around to reduce risk. Those who are looking to create sustainable income growth look to create multiple income streams and we often talk about diversification of passive and active income streams. This thinking is nothing new, it makes common sense. We do this because we want to reduce the risks should something go wrong. We understand that in diversifying we increase the scope of influence and increase productivity options.

Diversification in nature is also well known and critical to survival. We know that the natural world requires a range of inputs to thrive and survive. That isn't' to say that specialisation doesn't happen, it does, but such specialisations carry a high risk. Whilst the conditions are 'controlled' things are fine but what happens when things go wrong?

"One of nature's strengths lies in biodiversity. This helps to sustain it in the face of uncertainty. The value of portfolio diversification may have been reinvented by Harry Markowitz in the 1950s, but that lesson has been visible in the natural world for millions of years." (Hutchinson, 2021)

So, the language of diversification makes sense, we get it.

But what is it about the word diversity that is so hard to understand? Let alone put into practice.

Why, after all this time are we still having to have the conversation and push for real action?

Consider for a moment what your immediate thought is when you hear the word diversity; what do you picture? Is it racial, gender, sexuality, cultural manifestation of difference? Certainly, in the media and in corporate reports we hear words "let's celebrate our diversity" and "we have created diversity by getting people from different backgrounds on our board".

The focus seems to be on how much difference have we got so that others can see we are 'good'. But in business and in life, diversity isn't about how many different faces you have put in place. It isn't about a token display of difference, and it certainly isn't a PR exercise.

If we are genuine in our desire to value diversity, then what is needed is a shift in mindset and commitment through action. It is a fundamental reframing of how we make decisions for those we serve. It is a recognition that it is only through diversity that we will remain sustainable into the future. We need more than a 'different face', instead real diversity requires a fundamental shift in power that embraced difference in thought, interest, and curiosity. Because business, like life, will always be vulnerable to elements beyond our control. And if we put all our eggs in the one basket we may miss the opportunity for change, and we may very well stagnate.

What needs to be articulated is that diversity is more than a physical point of difference, real diversity embraces diversity of thought as much a diversity in being. When we create meaning to the language of diversity, we make it more accessible for people, we can reduce the reactive response to fear.

We know the research and evidence shows us that diversity helps create successful businesses (https://whattobecome.com/blog/diversity-in-the-workplace-statistics/) but did you also know that diversity helps us make better decisions? "According to **McKinsey & Company research**, businesses in the top quartile for gender diversity are 15% more likely to outperform their peers, and businesses in the top quartile for ethnic diversity are 35% more likely to outperform their peers." (Sucich, 2022) But perhaps more interestingly, "while homogeneity may lull people into thinking they are making better decisions (because everyone agrees with each other), viewpoints that challenge each other sharpen the performance of teams". (Sucich, 2022)

What diversity does, is provide an increased potential for different ideas, information, thoughts, perceptions and influences our decision-making in a more board, diverse and challenging way. When we have diversity of thought – we are less likely to group think, less prone to unconscious and bias influence.

By its very nature – diversity is about bringing difference into the room, allowing it to influence what information we have and how we assess and translate our decisions into action.

But here is a truth not often spoken of.

Difference also brings a higher potential for conflict.

It's because many of us don't deal with difference very well and at its heart, diversity is about difference. It is much easier when we all agree and think alike. It is safe, controlled, predictable. People fear difference, they fear losing control or power, they fear the unknown and don't want to feel uncomfortable. People also don't like change and avoid the problem rather than risk upsetting others, getting it wrong or looking bad.

As a result, problems turn into conflict.

Consider for a moment that conflict costs UK employers an estimated 28.5 billion (ACAS, 2021) pounds annually and in the US is costing companies $359 billion annually (Global, 2008). I know first-hand the impact of conflict, but I also know that so often the conflicts have arisen because of the inability to deal with difference. People can't seem to find a way to lean into these differences and instead turn them into a battle to be won, a positional debate where the winner takes all.

When we don't embrace diversity as an opportunity the costs are usually high, if not immediately then certainly in the longer term.

If we are to actualise diversity we also need to empower people to better deal with difference. We need to teach them how to have a difficult conversation without the need for a fight, learning that we can disagree without the need for a battle.

This here is at the heart of making diversity real.

Bringing diversity into the 'room' requires a sharing of power and influence and without a doubt takes more work. It requires that we wrestle with the messiness of humanity, that we collaborate and are willing to acknowledge the value of difference. When we understand this, we can better understand the resistance to meaningful diversity.

The reality is that embedding diversity not as tokenism but as function is hard, challenging work, but it gets easier with practice.

"Among groups where all three original members didn't already know the correct answer, adding an outsider versus an insider actually doubled their chance of arriving at the correct solution, from 29% to 60%. The work felt harder, but the outcomes were better." (Sucich, 2022)

In 2014 I enrolled in a cross-cultural leadership and peace-making project called Mawul Rom, in Galiwin'ku in the Northern Territory. This is where I really learnt the practical realities of what it means to lean into diversity and make it real – in our thoughts, our actions, and our results. In the governance of the project, our board, made up of Yolngu and Balanda members had to wrestle with the business of complex decision making done with mutual respect. We embraced cultural, gender and professional diversity and some days we did this well and other days were difficult. What allowed us to embrace our diversity was the underlying respect and trust in our shared relationships. When our trust wasn't aligned, decision making lost its integrity. We also understood the extent of our authority and our boundaries (what was and wasn't ok). When things got hard, and they did, it was our ability to be curious, seek understanding mutually of the interests and needs that enabled us to make the best decisions.

Honestly, the decisions made just in the Balanda space (as a

Balanda) were easier. We knew what we were dealing with, we all had shared experiences and could readily fill the gaps with assumed knowledge. But there were times when we didn't align, this was generally when value and interest diverged. I would imagine the same was true for Yolngu. However, it was the intersection space between cultures, the places of diversity, that were hardest to navigate. It took a willingness to be vulnerable and it took courage. There is a rawness that exists in this space – a space of not having all the answers. It took longer as we had to dive deep into the layers beneath the positions. I also know that when we made decisions in this way – even when they were hard or painful, they were the right decisions. There was a deep sense of peace, that we had made the right collective decision. These were the moments when diversity enhanced what we did and enabled us to make a long-term difference.

The more we leaned into the functionality of diversity, the better we got at making good decisions. We danced the relationship between diversity and decision-making in thought and in action.

So, I know that diversity matters. It matters as it allows us to grow forward in a way that embraces and uplifts people rather than diminishes them. When we get diversity right, we make decisions based on *diversification* of information, we are better able to assess risk and problem solve in a way that is much more creative and sustainable.

In know that because I have seen the rich rewards when people are able to come together to explore, negotiate and innovate their way beyond difference and really capitalise on the diversity of our humanity in business, and in life generally.

But what are the actions that can be taken to make diversity real? It means bringing difference into the place of decision-making, in both who we are and how we are. We need our business leaders to turn words in to function. We can capitalise on diversity and empower our decision-making by considering things like.

- Are we making decisions in a collaborative or dismiss way?
- Are we encouraging questions, curiosity, and difference?
- Do we lean into confusion, difference and conflict or do we avoid it?

We also to recognise that if we are to make diversity 'common sense' then we need to adjust the types of leaders we promote, employ, and raise up. Leaders who bring more than technical skills and industry experience, we need leaders who can elevate the people dynamics. This means considering principles, values, and competencies like:

- Power – leaders who see power as something to share rather than a way to control is more likely to embrace diversity.
- Courage – leadership who can 'park' their ego and be vulnerable, real, and honest are more likely to make space for difference.
- Emotional Intelligence – leaders who not only manage their own emotions but are able to manage others are better able to whether difficult conversations.
- Curiosity – these are the leaders who asks questions and are better problems solvers.

These leaders listen better to diversity and are more likely to make space for difference. They see diversity not as a threat but rather a key contributing factor to innovation and growth. But guess what, we all have the potential to be leaders in our own spaces. Ultimately diversity, real practical and sustainable diversity starts with each of us. When we bring an open, growth mindset we are better able to deeply understand that difference isn't a bad thing, instead it is our ability to lean into this with respect that launches us up!

Diversity in business requires courage to really embrace our differences of thinking to resolve, innovate and thrive. This is where the real work of functionality begins – the implementation of diversity in how we make critical decisions for our business. Diversity or diversification of who makes decisions and how we make decisions makes people sense, financial sense, and sustainable sense.

Bibliography

ACAS. (2021, May 11). *Estimating the costs of workplace conflict* . Retrieved from ACAS - working for everyone: https://www.acas.org.uk/estimating-the-costs-of-workplace-conflict-report

Brookesia Micra. (2022, August 26). Retrieved from Wikipedia: https://en.wikipedia.org/wiki/Brookesia_micra

Global, C. (2008 , July). *CPP Global Human Capital Report*. Retrieved from CPP Global : http://img.en25.com/Web/CPP/Conflict_report.pdf

Hutchinson, H. (2021, July 14). *On nature and diversification* . Retrieved from www.investec.com: https://www.investec.com/en_gb/focus/harolds-herald/on-nature-and-diversification.html

Sucich, K. (2022, February 15). *Why diversity matters in decision-making* . Retrieved from Dimensional Insight : https://www.dimins.com/blog/2022/02/15/diversity-matters-in-decision-making/

Brown, B. (2021) Atlas of the Heart: mapping meaningful connection and the language of the human heart, Penguin Random House, New York.

Website Referenced:

- https://www.forbes.com/sites/eriklarson/2017/09/21/new-research-diversity-inclusion-better-decision-making-at-work/?sh=6153e6ab4cbf
- https://www.mckinsey.com/featured-insights/diversity-and-inclusion/diversity-wins-how-inclusion-matters
- https://hbr.org/2016/09/diverse-teams-feel-less-comfortable-and-thats-why-they-perform-better
- https://brenebrown.com

Sarah Blake

Award-winning conflict strategist and mediator, TEDx speaker and bestselling author, Sarah Blake, elevates leaders, empowering them to overcome conflict barriers. Bringing clarity to complex decision-making during confusion, conflict and crisis, she helps transform problems into opportunities.

As a second-generation mediator with over twenty-six years of experience, Sarah has engaged in some of the most complex problem situations across remote Australia and into the Pacific. She has worked within corporate, university and NFP sectors delivering intervention and is increasingly sought by leaders struggling with the impact of conflict and change.

Working across industries has provided opportunities to engage with bodies such as the World Bank, BHP, Australian Federal Police, Land Councils and national, state and local government.

Sarah has delivered talks across the world, both in person and online, and is considered a thought leader within the industry. This has enabled her to contribute to international advisory boards and support the development of the next generation of peacemakers.

She is an accredited mediator with Resolution Institute and International Mediation Institute and is the Australian Ambassador for Mediate Guru and an Ambassador for Think Network UK. Sarah is also a multiple-bestselling author and regular contributor to media in Australia including television, radio and print where she is talking all things conflict from growth leaderships, people dynamics and culture.

The Power of Women Leading the Way to Economic Development

Kelly Markey

Mzansi is an informal name for South Africa. My official birthland. A country that has so many wounds that puncture deeper than anyone cares to know, cloaked with scars that are more aching than bleeding.

In 1994, my first employment in South Africa was for the federal government providing health care in a primary care clinic. The South African health system and funding is nothing like the developed world. One fine day, jubilant under the African overcast sky, I rocked up to work with a spring in my step, young and all euthanasic. The waiting room was overcrowded with mothers, toddlers, babies and other patients. The sweltering heat and lack of air conditioning made the cries of numerous children amplified, the flies and body odour from poor hygiene created a vortex for my office space, and yet another day at work … in my stride.

A group of children were fussing like chicks around a brooding mother hen, nothing abnormal, yet the picture looked distorted. Eventually it was this mother's turn to check in for the clinic's health services, and I was serving her. She had seven kids all due for mandatory immunisation, and they were also malnourished. In accordance to organisation protocol, we had to weigh each child. Only if a child registered below the poverty line, a food hamper was distributed. I weighed the first five children; they did not qualify. The mother was already pleading with me in native vernacular to help her with food to sustain her kids. The calculated ambiguity knocked right into reality when she placed her sixth child on the scale. He was just skin and bones.

Do not underestimate someone who has to sacrifice a family member in order for their family to survive; it tells a story of their soul. Social intelligence finds a way to unravel the beast in a cage of an unfair economy. Some mothers are broken in places that you did not even know existed – enduring and unseen. Life marches on swiftly for those that are chasing dreams and status. This mother had to innovate a model of care to sustain her family – starve one child to feed the rest! In my considered opinion, the system is flawed. No human should be in a predicament to make an economic decision to starve a child in the name of survival. This is an economy that is vastly brutal. I tried to thread the needle and confirmed yes, your child qualifies for the hamper. As I walked away to fetch the it, tears gushed down my cheeks knowing all too well that this child was just a heartbeat away from death. Miserably, there will be many more sacrificed in an unjust economy. It's inhumane to watch the plight of humans.

Chronic financial struggle lends itself to mortal trials and tribulations. I want to believe that this mother's heart is as soft and warm as a fur coat as she walks away with her seven kids.

Cradling her malnourished child, gazing at him with tears uncontrollably gushing forth. Our eyes lock yet again – she reads my heart, I blink and tears fall – she walks away. This mama ate out of her personality. A personality that explored every economic option to feed her family. I chose to respond rather than react. I had seen this form of cruel intervention in the name of survival. Mothers chose to starve one of their children so they could qualify for a food hamper to feed the rest of the family.

Not a moment to console myself, and the next momma is eagerly waiting her turn. Her child is a healthy weight and as a result does not qualify for a food hamper. She starts wailing in an amplified tone. I calmly explain the situation to her. Our world is vitriolic. I need to move on to the next patient. Everyday work is not just history, but I am part of the fabric of this history for so many humans. This woman knows the economy is going to claim her child as well, so she dashed around the corner and pushed her way into the door of my office.

My first encounter with kwashiorkor, a form of severe protein malnutrition characterised by edema and an enlarged liver with fatty infiltrates. Inadequate food supply is correlated with occurrences of kwashiorkor; occurrences in high-income countries are rare. It occurs amongst weaning children to ages of about five years old. The unpleasant anxiety advanced into a subtle stalemate as I looked the mother in her eyes, she feels decidedly unwell but she holds my gaze. I am angry and it's painted on my face. With an acute and well-accomplished attitude of askance the mother asked me if her child qualified for the food hamper. With a complete look that speaks of nothing but survival. I am not angry at her; she is just trying to survive – the world at large has ways of dealing with the economy as if no human lives are part of the equation.

A healthy distraction to introduce a feeding scheme mandated by parameters for humans to qualify. Then there is an exception to the rule: a child who has kwashiorkor seriously requires proper nutrition but the system prevents it because his symptoms created a pot belly and his weight does not win him the prize to live. With intention and solution, we may have a vocal hero but the sick aspects are, the landscape is festered with so many victims. This mother refused to give up on her child, she was now in my office prostrate on the floor holding my ankles crying, pleading, begging for me to help a child. I have no words to describe the emotions that unleashed. Watching a mother trapped in an economy that gave her no hope for a future but to fall on her face and beg for survival – this is the real policy that was stamped on my heart this hectic and philosophical day. My hand was tied to help her in accordance to organisation policy ... what a sad business operation.

How can I perform my job optimally when every patient unravels a fountain of tears? I resolved to not let unconditional love die on my watch. I grabbed my handbag and gave her all my cash to buy food. Past and present has sprouted the philanthropist in me. I am acutely aware that this solution of helping an individual does not provide a scaled answer to the problem. I would rather be the person that brings hope to one individual and stop them from crying, even if it's just for a minute. No economy can heal itself when we deliberately choose to look away and pretend someone somewhere will make a material difference. It is evident that policy and the whole gamut is moving at glacier speed ... do you really want humans to be trapped in this web?

The power of women leading the way to economic development begins with looking a woman in the eyes when she is begging for the survival of her children and not pointing her to a flawed system, but rather prescribing the fragrance of assurance no matter how glim it is.

With the progression of twenty-nine years, not much has changed. Policy, lawmakers, political agendas and an unhealthy dose of corruption has marched nowhere close to fill the gap. Thanks to these facts of my first-hand experience the inconvenient truth lives. Nothing is even keeled in African society today. Woman are still forced to find innovative ways to combat issues that they did not bargain for. The world is not scarce on memorabilia but the solutions are not just the same. Health pundits look at you like a rookie – a small fish in a big pond. My motto is to look where you are going, not where society stagnates. Help where I can. I am fortunate enough to be exposed to the educational and corporate systems in South Africa, New Zealand, Singapore and Australia. These platforms have given me capabilities, expertise and insights. I have also encountered many characters who exhibit the loquacious essence but rarely lift a finger to be part of the solution. Let's wake up and smell the coffee. We are not going to get reform on a global level from those that are at the top of the food chain. The onus is upon you and me to make a quantifiable modification.

Work at grassroot levels. Address issues at community level. Then, via for the bottled neck policy, change on national and global horizon. If you are serious about shrinking the gap in our current economy, then capture your bedrock vision and put it into action. We are called to make a visible distinction to our global economic growth and we can do this when we endow each other opportunities to shine brighter and carve a better life and future in a practical and all-inclusive manner. Peppering your path with agape love, encouragement and dispensing the aroma of hope. You have eyes that see and a heart that comprehends that life is not always easy for everyone. Our economy is not balanced, some tides are unfair, others are distorted with intention and so many are trapped in a vortex with no chance at all. Kindness still exists and faith with action can move those mountains. Veer off the beaten path and look for an approach that brings promise. Stumble around if you have to, but find a meaningful way to navigate transformation. Staring at the summit energies grit – unleash your tenacity.

I work as a health executive in the information technology platform. This space has offered me the opportunity to impact the global economy in a profound manner. I have designed, enhanced and implemented some of the world's greatest innovative systems to advance our clinical footprint. I will zoom into this in another book ... stay tuned. The acronym KPI usually equates to Key Performance Indicators. From my vast array of experience in the corporate, social, cultural, spiritual and international bestselling author hats I know that without a shadow of doubt that most mothers in Africa will fail the KPI's that are mandated for motherhood in the developed world. In reality these women deserve a standing ovation, we need to salute them for finding ways in an economy that is designed to never give them a chance to be a normal mother. An impartial and inclusive acronym would be Keep People Inspired or Keep People Interested. This is a recipe for a thriving economy. Self-assured mothers produce optimistic children, which impacts our economy in dramatic ways.

What is the purpose of getting mentors to help you earn another stripe to pin on your lapel. The real badge of honour is respecting lives, saving lives and changing the narrative. The external economy can benefit from your personal brand when you set the benchmark. Are you accountable? Are you reachable? Have you assumed responsibility for something greater than yourself and your gene pool? Does the calibre of your brand spread the season of sustained optimism? What makes you distinctively different? When did you bring encouragement to a bleak situation? What is the most prominent experience you had that impacted another person profoundly by your deeds? As woman of distinction, we are entrusted with an ethical fundamental to revamp, remodel and recalibrate our tactic towards women empowerment and how it correlates to our economy. Sourcing and proper provision are the fundamental building blocks to bridge the gap and save lives, how are you helping with this? Many women would attest to the fact that a big piece of their identity slips away when they become mothers. Yet somehow in some way they also discover who they are. Every mother should be afforded the beauty to dabble and find their sure foot but never ever be mandated to sell her soul.

Bringing balance to our economy it's not just about metrics it's about transformed mindset, social norms and institutions that still hinder women empowerment. One of the global issues is that we are not looking at business intelligence data and drilling down to a level to obtain a real picture at micro level. Why is the gender gap still gaping at us? Why is the wage cavity still on the shelf? Even when most countries have sound policies and enforceable legislation for the promotion of gender equality the telling tale is what really happens behind closed doors. This is what we need to address, why does policy and legislation fail? Just because something becomes a policy it does not equate to success, period. We are the agents that will bring the element of success. Education is funnelled in accordance to gender. This adversely affects females as they are deemed homemakers and don't get the opportunity to gain basic skills for economic evolution. Social norms of women been the carer puts her at a disadvantage. Humanity needs a plan for sustainable development, we need to combat the limitations of unpaid work in the home. We need to open the horizon to digital transformation giving equal opportunity for women even in rural homes. A plethora of training, tele health, domestic violence combats and other options can be deployed digitally and in local language.

A telling tale emerges from gender response procurement – be more strategic about who you are giving the opportunities to. The month of August is declared woman's month in South Africa. A conscious decision to bridge the gap. In 2022, South Africa implemented 40% preferences for female-lead businesses. Women make up 58% of Africa's self-employed population and contribute around 13% of the continent's GDP. Until gender parity is improved throughout the African continent, female entrepreneurs will remain under-earning compared with their male counterparts. Governments and policymakers can support women entrepreneurs and female led start-ups in Africa through targeted policies including gender-responsive budgeting and utilizing the African Continental Free Trade Agreement. This is the start in correct direction, however sadly nepotism and corruption derail the vision. History paints a clear picture for us to heed from and move forward with precision.

Statistics reveal that woman who are supported, enhance the community and economy. When we ignore what women carry the economy will not accelerate on auto pilot. The incorrect interpretation of risk will always be the silent enemy. When the public and private sector are limited then new blood needs to arise from women who realize the demand to change the narrative. Chart a pathway to remove the barriers. Create partnerships with organisations that are gender transformative, take time to assess the contract, values and mission statement before you sign any deal – request a realignment to ensure your strategic values are met. Observe how an organisation treats woman that are employed by them. Ensure durable design lens are used to empower economic framework proactively. Social standards, country economy is varied, value chain is never the same and culture impacts outcomes so a one size fits all mandate will not suffice. Ask the crucial questions about how solutions are tailored. Request access to toolkits used by organizations to become gender transformative. Get beneath the hood and take a look.

We are living in a digital era yet substantial households still do not have power connection.

Psychological needs are the most basic human needs such as hunger thirst and shelter no human should beg for this! Try new things in order to achieve better results. Once a picture of revolt now equates to a sense of resolve when **YOU** decide to be in the equation. We are in the twenty-first century yet we are haunted and vexed by policy-makers, enforcement organisations and personal agendas that support sex slaves and murder in the name of policing dress code. The reality is that women are themselves traded as commodities. The slave trade, human trafficking and cultural dictations set a pace for the economy and fracture the wellbeing of woman. Jeffrey Epstein's sex trafficking activities illustrate how vulnerable woman are. In 2022, the world watched the conflict zone in Iran after the death of Masha Amini. Our economy churns with lives that matter ... does your prejudice mast vast assumptions about your capabilities as your actions or lack of zeal also contributes to the same economy. We are all as strong as the weakest link!

Reference

1. Reference to Kwashiorkor, https://en.wikipedia.org/wiki/Kwashiorkor
2. Reference to female start-ups https://www.weforum.org/agenda/2022/08/how-female-led-start-ups-can-transform-africa/

Kelly Markey

Kelly Markey is a highly accomplished professional with over thirty years of experience in the health industry. She has worked all over the world for major world gorillas and has gained extensive knowledge and expertise by travelling to over two hundred cities. Expertly equipped from her richly-lived experience, she is an accomplished writer whose books, including *Don't Just Fly, Soar* and *Glean, Grow and Glow*, have become bestsellers. In addition to her impressive career achievements, Kelly is also dedicated to philanthropy, supporting numerous organizations around the globe that work towards women's empowerment and spiritual growth. With her electrifying presentations that are renowned for motivating, educating, and inspiring audiences to reach new heights, Kelly truly shines as a leader in her field.

Kelly is a passionate advocate for social justice and equality. She works tirelessly to raise awareness about racism and discrimination, utilizing her unique platform as a prominent women's leader and cover girl to facilitate important conversations about these crucial issues. Kelly has been featured on numerous radio stations, newspapers and magazines around the world, and she speaks five different languages.

Through her advocacy work, Kelly aims to reduce the trauma and ignorance associated with racism and discrimination by promoting positive mental health and providing opportunities for dialogue. Her commitment to these issues is truly inspiring, and she continues to be a role model for women everywhere. Whether she is rocking the stage at an international conference or speaking out in the media, Kelly is an unstoppable force for good in our world today.

Whether you need guidance on your personal or professional life, Kelly Markey is the go-to expert you can trust. As a result of her work, Kelly has helped countless individuals to achieve their dreams and reach their full potential.

Why Diversity is the New Way of Doing Business in Technology

HE Laila Rahhal EL ATFANI

In recent years, there has been a growing movement to promote diversity in all workplaces, but especially in the technology sector. This is because the industry has long been dominated by white males, and women and other minorities have often been excluded from leadership positions.

There are several reasons why diversity is important in the tech industry. For one, it can help to create products and services that are more inclusive of all users. Additionally, a more diverse workforce can bring different perspectives and skill sets to the table, which can lead to more innovative solutions.

There are several ways to promote diversity in the tech industry. One is to increase the number of women and minority employees at all levels of an organization. Another is to create mentorship and networking programs to help women and minorities advance in their careers. Additionally, companies can provide training on unconscious bias and create policies that promote diversity.

Technology companies that embrace diversity will be better positioned to succeed in the future. A more diverse workforce can bring new perspectives and ideas to the table, which can lead to more innovative products and services. In addition, customers will increasingly expect companies to reflect their values, and those that fail to do so may lose business. Promoting diversity can help attract and retain top talent, as women and minorities are increasingly seeking out workplaces that are inclusive and supportive.

Women leaders in technology are increasingly championing diversity as the new way of doing business. In a male-dominated industry, they are recognizing the importance of creating an inclusive environment that embraces different perspectives and backgrounds. By doing so, they are opening new opportunities for innovation and creativity.

In a rapidly changing world, technology companies need to be agile and adaptable to survive. Women leaders who embrace diversity are helping to position their companies for success in the future. As the UAE and Australia move towards becoming leading hubs for deep tech, they are setting the stage for a more diverse and inclusive tech industry. Women leaders who embrace diversity are at the forefront of this shift, and they are poised to lead the way in the years to come.

Diversity is not only important in the workplace, but it is also necessary for a successful society. A society that embraces diversity is one that is accepting and open-minded, which leads to progress and innovation. Women leaders who prioritize diversity are helping to move our society in this positive direction, and they should be applauded for their efforts.

Some additional statistics that support the idea that embracing diversity leads to better financial performance include:

A study by McKinsey & Company found that companies with more gender diversity on their executive teams were 33% more likely to experience above-average profitability. Another study by Credit Suisse found that companies with at least one female board member generated returns on equity that were 10.1% higher than those of companies without any women on their boards. And finally, a report by Ernst & Young showed that businesses with greater ethnic and cultural diversity outperform their peers financially. This is likely because having a variety of perspectives allows organizations to identify new opportunities and respond to challenges in a more innovative way.

HE Laila Rahhal ELATFANI

Her Excellency Laila Rahhal El Atfani is a globally respected women empowerment advocate and successful businesswoman. She has won multiple awards for her work in business and promoting gender equality. She is a powerful role model for women and is passionate about promoting the girl child.

Her expertise in women empowerment has seen her keynote speeches at various global conferences on the subject. As a successful businesswoman, she offers invaluable advice to other women looking to start or grow their businesses. Her experience in digital transformation makes her ideally placed to advise businesses on how to make the most of new technologies.

Her Excellency Laila Rahhal El Atfani is also heavily involved in charity work, helping those less fortunate than herself. She is the President and Founder of Business Gate, and I Am Africa platform organisations which aim to help empower women and young people across Africa. She is also the head of diplomacy and protocol for AACID (Arab African Council For integration and Development

And WPC (World peace committee 202).

Her passion for empowering women, and youth has seen her establish the 'I Am Africa Platform which provides opportunities and platforms to all entrepreneurs in Africa. The foundation has helped thousands of youths to become job creators and go on to lead successful lives.

Her Excellency Laila Rahhal El Atfani is a powerful role model for women across the world.